Wrocław

Travel Guide 2023

Exploring a City Steeped in History

Fernando A. Carlos

TABLE OF CONTENTS

Wroclaw visitation story

During my recent trip to Poland, I had the pleasure of visiting the beautiful city of Wroclaw. Known for its picturesque architecture, rich history, and vibrant culture, Wroclaw proved to be an enchanting destination that left a lasting impression on me. My visit began with a stroll through the city's historic center, where I was immediately captivated by the stunning Gothic architecture that graced the streets. The iconic Market Square, with its colorful facades and intricate details, stood as the heart of Wroclaw and instantly transported me back in time. I couldn't help but admire the impressive Town Hall, which stood tall and proud, dominating the square.

As I explored the city further, I discovered the delightful Ostrow Tumski, also known as Cathedral Island. This small district, nestled on the banks of the Oder River, was a serene oasis of tranquility. The magnificent Wroclaw Cathedral, with its soaring towers and intricate stained glass windows, provided a sense of awe-inspiring beauty. I spent a peaceful afternoon wandering through the cobblestone streets, admiring the charming houses and crossing over the Tumski Bridge while taking in the picturesque views. One of the highlights of my visit was undoubtedly the enchanting Wroclaw's Dwarfs, or "Krasnale." These tiny bronze statues could be found scattered throughout the city, adding a touch of whimsy to every corner. Each dwarf had its own unique character and story, representing various aspects of Wroclaw's history and culture. I made it my mission to find as many of them as possible, and it became a delightful scavenger hunt that led me to hidden alleys, tucked-away squares, and unexpected surprises.

In the evening, I immersed myself in Wroclaw's vibrant nightlife. The city came alive with energy as locals and tourists alike filled the cozy bars and bustling restaurants. I indulged in delicious Polish cuisine, savoring pierogi, hearty stews, and mouthwatering desserts. The warm hospitality of the locals made me feel welcome, and I found myself engaging in lively conversations, exchanging stories and laughter until the late hours. No visit to Wroclaw would be complete without crossing one of its many bridges. The iconic Grunwaldzki Bridge, adorned with its impressive architecture and decorative sculptures, offered breathtaking views of the cityscape and the flowing river below. Standing there, watching the sun set over Wroclaw, I couldn't help but feel a sense of awe and gratitude for the opportunity to experience such a remarkable place.

As my time in Wroclaw came to an end, I realized that this city had left an indelible mark on my heart. Its blend of history, art, and vibrant atmosphere had captured my imagination and made me fall in love with its charm. Wroclaw had truly surpassed my expectations and became a destination I would always cherish in my memories. Whether it was wandering through its ancient streets, marveling at its architectural wonders, or simply enjoying the warm embrace of its people, Wroclaw offered a captivating experience that I would recommend to any traveler seeking a taste of Polish culture and beauty.

History of Wroclaw

The history of Wroclaw is a rich tapestry that spans over a thousand years, filled with tales of conquest, resilience, and cultural exchange. Situated in western Poland, Wroclaw has experienced the influences of various empires and civilizations throughout its existence, shaping its unique identity. The origins of Wroclaw can be traced back to the 9th century when a Slavic tribe known as the Wrocławi settled in the area. The settlement flourished and developed into a regional center of trade and commerce. In 990, Wroclaw became the capital of the newly established Polish state, under the rule of Duke Mieszko I.

Over the centuries, Wroclaw changed hands several times. In 1241, it was devastated by the Mongols during their invasion of Poland. However, the city quickly recovered and entered a period of prosperity under the reign of the Piast dynasty. In the 14th century, Wroclaw joined the Hanseatic League, a powerful trading alliance that brought wealth and influence to the city.

In 1335, Wroclaw became part of the Kingdom of Bohemia, under the rule of the Czech monarchs. This marked the beginning of a new era for the city, as it adopted German influence and culture, which would shape its development for centuries to come. The Germanic influence intensified during the reign of the Habsburg dynasty, who incorporated Wroclaw into the Austrian Empire in 1526.

During the 16th and 17th centuries, Wroclaw experienced significant growth and became a center of intellectual and artistic achievements. It attracted scholars, artists, and craftsmen from various parts of Europe, contributing to the city's reputation as a hub of culture and learning. The University of Wroclaw, founded in 1702, played a pivotal role in this intellectual flourishing. The 19th century brought significant changes to Wroclaw as it became part of the Kingdom of Prussia following the Napoleonic Wars. Under Prussian rule, the city underwent industrialization and modernization, transforming into a major industrial center with a thriving textile industry. The German population grew, and the city's architecture reflected the neo-Gothic and neo-Renaissance styles prevalent in Germany at the time. The aftermath of World War I saw a shift in power dynamics, and Wroclaw became part of the newly established Republic of Poland in 1919. The city, however, retained its predominantly German population. Tensions between the Polish and German communities escalated in the years leading up to World War II.

Following the war, Wroclaw underwent a dramatic transformation. The German population was expelled, and the city was repopulated with Polish settlers. Many historic buildings were damaged or destroyed during the war, but significant efforts were made to rebuild and restore the city's architectural heritage. Wroclaw became a cultural and industrial center in post-war Poland, attracting investment and fostering a vibrant arts scene.

In recent decades, Wroclaw has experienced rapid growth and development, emerging as a major economic and cultural hub in Central Europe. It has hosted international events such as the European Football Championship and the World Games, further solidifying its position on the global stage.

Today, Wroclaw stands as a testament to the resilience of its people and the power of cultural exchange. Its rich history is visible in its diverse architecture, blending Gothic, Renaissance, and Baroque styles, and its vibrant cultural scene continues to thrive, making it a captivating destination for visitors from around the world.

Welcome to Wroclaw

Welcome to Wroclaw, a city that will captivate you with its history, charm, and vibrant atmosphere. Situated in western Poland, Wroclaw is a destination that seamlessly blends the old with the new, offering visitors a unique and unforgettable experience.

As you arrive in Wroclaw, you'll be greeted by a city that embraces both tradition and modernity. The historic center, with its cobbled streets and splendid architecture, will transport you back in time. The Market Square, Rynek, is the heart of Wroclaw and a perfect starting point for your exploration. Admire the colorful facades of the buildings, marvel at the Gothic beauty of the Town Hall, and soak in the lively ambiance of this bustling square.

Wroclaw's Dwarfs, or "Krasnale," will undoubtedly capture your attention. These whimsical bronze statues are scattered throughout the city, waiting to be discovered. Each dwarf has its own unique character and story, adding a touch of magic and playfulness to your visit. Keep an eye out for them as you explore the city, and see how many you can find!

As you venture beyond the historic center, you'll discover a city that embraces cultural diversity. Wroclaw is home to a vibrant arts scene, with numerous galleries, theaters, and music venues. The National Museum will take you on a journey through Polish history and art, while the Wroclaw Opera House offers enchanting performances. Food lovers will delight in Wroclaw's culinary offerings. Indulge in traditional Polish cuisine, from hearty pierogi (dumplings) to flavorful Polish sausages. Don't forget to try the local specialty, żurek, a sour rye soup that will tantalize your taste buds. Wroclaw's vibrant nightlife is not to be missed either, with a plethora of bars, clubs, and restaurants offering entertainment and a chance to mingle with locals and fellow travelers.

Nature enthusiasts will find respite in Wroclaw's beautiful parks and green spaces. Take a leisurely stroll along the Oder River or visit the tranquil Szczytnicki Park, home to the breathtaking Japanese Garden. The

Centennial Hall, a UNESCO World Heritage Site, is a testament to Wroclaw's architectural prowess and a must-see for history and design enthusiasts.

Wroclaw is a city of festivals and events, offering a vibrant calendar throughout the year. From music festivals and cultural celebrations to Christmas markets and street performances, there is always something happening in Wroclaw that will leave you with unforgettable memories. But perhaps what truly makes Wroclaw special is its warm and welcoming atmosphere. The locals, known for their friendliness and hospitality, will make you feel right at home. Engage in conversations, learn about their traditions, and embrace the vibrant spirit of this remarkable city.

So, welcome to Wroclaw, where history, culture, and a warm embrace await you. Get ready to immerse yourself in an unforgettable experience that will leave you enchanted and longing to return. Enjoy your stay in this magnificent city that effortlessly weaves together the past and the present, creating a tapestry of beauty and inspiration.

Geography and climate of Wroclaw

Wroclaw, located in western Poland, is a city with a diverse geography and a moderate continental climate. Its position along the Oder River contributes to its scenic beauty and plays a role in shaping its climate.

Geographically, Wroclaw is situated in the Lower Silesian Lowland, which is characterized by relatively flat terrain. The city is surrounded by picturesque landscapes, including rolling hills, fertile farmland, and charming river valleys. The Oder River, flowing through Wroclaw, adds a distinctive element to the city's geography, providing opportunities for leisure activities and enhancing its natural beauty. Wroclaw experiences a moderate continental climate, influenced by its inland location and proximity to the Carpathian Mountains. Summers in Wroclaw are generally warm and humid, with temperatures averaging around 20 to 25 degrees Celsius (68 to 77 degrees Fahrenheit). It is the sunniest season, with long daylight hours and occasional thunderstorms. Spring and autumn bring mild temperatures, ranging from 10 to 20 degrees Celsius (50 to 68 degrees Fahrenheit), and are characterized by changing foliage and pleasant weather for outdoor activities.

Winter in Wroclaw can be cold, with temperatures often dropping below freezing. The average winter temperature ranges from -5 to 2 degrees Celsius (23 to 36 degrees Fahrenheit). Snowfall is common during this season, transforming the city into a winter wonderland. It's worth noting that the weather conditions in Wroclaw can vary from year to year, with some winters being milder or harsher than others.

Precipitation in Wroclaw is fairly evenly distributed throughout the year, although slightly higher levels can be expected in the summer months. Rainfall is generally moderate, and snowfall is common during the winter months. The city experiences approximately 700 to 800 millimeters (27 to 31 inches) of precipitation annually.

The diverse geography of Wroclaw and its surrounding areas offers opportunities for outdoor activities such as hiking, cycling, and boating. The Oder River and its numerous islands provide a scenic backdrop for leisurely walks and water-based adventures.

Wroclaw's geography and climate combine to create a city that offers a pleasant and varied experience throughout the year. From enjoying outdoor festivals in the summer to exploring snowy landscapes in the winter, visitors to Wroclaw can embrace the beauty of its geography and adapt to its changing seasons.

Iconic landmarks and hidden gems in Wroclaw

Wroclaw, with its rich history and vibrant culture, is home to a plethora of iconic landmarks and hidden gems waiting to be discovered. From historic sites that showcase the city's heritage to off-the-beaten-path treasures, here are some of the must-see attractions in Wroclaw.

Wroclaw Market Square (Rynek)

Wroclaw Market Square, known as Rynek in Polish, is the vibrant heart of the city and one of the largest medieval squares in Europe. Stepping into this bustling square is like entering a world frozen in time, where history merges seamlessly with the energy of modern life. The Market Square has been a central gathering place in Wroclaw since the city's founding in the 13th century. It served as a bustling marketplace, a venue for public events, and a social hub for locals and visitors alike. Today, it continues to be a vibrant center of activity, lined with colorful buildings, charming cafes, and bustling shops. At the heart of the Market Square stands the majestic Wroclaw Town Hall. This Gothic masterpiece is an architectural gem, featuring intricate details and soaring towers. Dating back to the 13th century, the Town Hall has been witness to the city's rich history and is a symbol of Wroclaw's resilience. Climb the tower to enjoy panoramic views of the city or step inside to explore the Wroclaw City Museum, which offers insights into the city's past. Surrounding the Market Square are rows of beautifully preserved historic buildings, each telling its own story. These architectural gems showcase various styles, including Gothic, Renaissance, and Baroque. Many of them are adorned with stunning facades, ornate details, and colorful paintwork, adding to the square's picturesque charm. The Market Square is not only a feast for the eyes but also a treat for the taste buds. Numerous cafes, restaurants, and food stalls offer a wide range of culinary delights, from traditional Polish cuisine to international flavors. Take a seat at an outdoor terrace and savor the flavors while immersing yourself in the lively atmosphere. Throughout the year, the Market Square hosts various events and festivals, adding an extra layer of excitement to the vibrant ambiance. From Christmas markets to music concerts and cultural celebrations, there is always something happening in this lively square. The atmosphere becomes even more enchanting during the holiday season when the square is adorned with festive decorations and filled with the joyful spirit of Christmas. The Market Square is also the perfect starting point for exploring the rest of Wroclaw. Its central location allows easy access to other attractions, such as the University of Wroclaw, the Ostrów Tumski district, and the Oder River embankment. Whether you visit during the day when the square is alive with activity or in the evening when it transforms into a magical setting with beautifully illuminated buildings, Wroclaw Market Square will leave a lasting impression. Its timeless charm, architectural splendor, and vibrant energy make it a must-see destination that truly captures the essence of this remarkable city.

Wroclaw Cathedral (Cathedral of St. John the Baptist)

The Wroclaw Cathedral, also known as the Cathedral of St. John the Baptist, is an awe-inspiring masterpiece and one of the most significant religious and architectural landmarks in Wroclaw, Poland. Situated on Cathedral Island (Ostrow Tumski), this majestic Gothic cathedral stands as a testament to the city's rich history and spiritual heritage. The history of the Wroclaw Cathedral dates back over a thousand years. The original church on this site was built in the 10th century and underwent numerous expansions and renovations over the centuries. The current cathedral, with its iconic twin towers, was constructed between the 13th and 15th centuries and exhibits remarkable Gothic architecture.

As you approach the cathedral, you'll be struck by its grandeur and imposing presence. The intricately carved facade, adorned with spires, gargoyles, and decorative elements, showcases the craftsmanship and attention to detail that went into its construction. The towering twin towers, reaching a height of around 98 meters (321 feet), dominate the skyline of Wroclaw and offer breathtaking panoramic views of the city from their summits. Step inside the cathedral, and you'll find yourself immersed in a world of architectural splendor and religious significance. The interior is characterized by soaring vaulted ceilings, ornate chapels, and stunning stained glass windows that filter light into a kaleidoscope of colors. The intricate stone carvings, sculptures, and decorative elements throughout the cathedral further exemplify the skill and artistry of the craftsmen who contributed to its creation. One of the most revered treasures housed within the Wroclaw Cathedral is the Gothic-style marble sarcophagus of St. Hedwig of Silesia, a revered figure in Polish history. The cathedral also contains numerous chapels, each with its own unique design and religious artifacts, offering visitors a glimpse into the spiritual significance of the site.

Climbing the cathedral's towers is an unforgettable experience. As you ascend the narrow spiral staircase, you'll be rewarded with panoramic views of Wroclaw's rooftops, the Oder River, and the surrounding landscape. The vistas are particularly stunning during sunset or when the city is blanketed in a layer of snow. The Wroclaw Cathedral holds significant cultural and religious importance, hosting religious ceremonies, concerts, and cultural events throughout the year. It is also a place of pilgrimage for both locals and tourists who seek solace, reflection, and a connection to the city's spiritual roots. Visiting the Wroclaw Cathedral is an opportunity to delve into the city's history, admire exquisite craftsmanship, and experience a sense of awe-inspiring beauty. Its architectural magnificence, combined with its religious and cultural significance, make it a must-see destination that leaves a lasting impression on all who visit.

University of Wroclaw

The University of Wroclaw, established in 1702, is one of the oldest and most prestigious universities in Poland

and Central Europe. Situated in the heart of Wroclaw, the university's rich history, architectural beauty, and academic excellence make it a significant cultural and educational institution in the city. The university's roots can be traced back to the Jesuit College, which was founded in 1655. However, it officially gained university status under the name Leopoldina University in 1702. The university was named after Emperor Leopold I of Austria, who granted the institution its charter. Throughout its history, the university has played a vital role in shaping intellectual and scientific pursuits in the region.

The architectural ensemble of the University of Wroclaw is a sight to behold. The main building, located on the University Square, is a magnificent example of Baroque architecture. The centerpiece of the complex is the Aula Leopoldina, a grand ceremonial hall renowned for its stunning frescoes, intricate stucco work, and ornate decor. The Aula Leopoldina is often considered one of the most beautiful Baroque halls in Europe. The university offers a wide range of academic disciplines and programs across its numerous faculties. These faculties cover a broad spectrum of fields, including humanities, natural sciences, social sciences, law, medicine, and more. The university's commitment to academic excellence is reflected in its faculty members, who are renowned experts in their respective fields. The University of Wroclaw is not just a place of education but also a hub of cultural and intellectual activities. Its library, with its vast collection of books and manuscripts, attracts scholars and researchers from around the world. The university's museums and galleries house significant art collections and historical artifacts, providing further avenues for exploration and learning.

The university's vibrant student community adds to its dynamic atmosphere. Students from various backgrounds come together to pursue their academic aspirations, participate in extracurricular activities, and engage in cultural and social events. The university also fosters international collaboration and exchange programs, welcoming students from different countries and promoting cultural diversity.

Beyond its academic pursuits, the University of Wroclaw is deeply embedded in the fabric of the city's history and culture. It serves as a cultural center, hosting lectures, conferences, concerts, and exhibitions that enrich the cultural landscape of Wroclaw. The university's influence extends far beyond its campus, shaping the intellectual and social development of the city and its inhabitants. Visiting the University of Wroclaw offers a glimpse into the intellectual heritage and academic excellence that define the city. Whether you explore its architectural marvels, engage with its vibrant student community, or immerse yourself in its intellectual atmosphere, the University of Wroclaw provides a window into the pursuit of knowledge and the spirit of innovation.

Centennial Hall

The Centennial Hall, also known as Hala Stulecia in Polish, is an architectural masterpiece and a UNESCO World Heritage Site located in Wroclaw, Poland. Designed by the renowned German architect Max Berg, this iconic structure is an outstanding example of early 20th-century reinforced concrete architecture and an enduring symbol of Wroclaw's cultural and historical significance. The construction of the Centennial Hall took place between 1911 and 1913, in commemoration of the 100th anniversary of Napoleon's defeat at the Battle of Leipzig. The hall was designed to serve as a multi-purpose venue for hosting exhibitions, trade fairs, concerts, and other large-scale events. It was intended to showcase Wroclaw's industrial and cultural achievements and to leave a lasting legacy for future generations. The Centennial Hall's architectural design is characterized by its innovative use of reinforced concrete, a pioneering technique at the time. The structure features a massive reinforced concrete dome with a diameter of 65 meters (213 feet) and a height of 42 meters (138 feet). This dome, with its intricate ribbed construction, stands as a testament to the architectural ingenuity and engineering skills of the era. Surrounding the hall is a circular colonnade adorned with decorative sculptures, creating an impressive and harmonious ensemble. The exterior of the Centennial Hall is embellished with intricate details, including friezes, reliefs, and ornamental motifs, showcasing the artistry and craftsmanship of the period.

Inside the Centennial Hall, you'll find a spacious and versatile interior. The main hall, with a capacity of over 7,000 people, is a grand space that can be adapted for various events. The hall's acoustics are renowned for their excellence, making it a favored venue for concerts and musical performances. Adjacent to the Centennial Hall is the Pergola, a picturesque architectural structure featuring lush gardens, fountains, and water features. The Pergola provides a tranquil space for relaxation and leisure, offering a beautiful contrast to the grandeur of the main hall. The Centennial Hall has been a witness to significant events throughout its history. It has hosted numerous exhibitions, concerts by renowned artists, and important political gatherings. One of its most notable events was the Congress of the Communist Party of Poland in 1948, which marked a turning point in the country's history.

Today, the Centennial Hall continues to be a vibrant cultural center in Wroclaw. It hosts a wide range of events, including concerts, theater performances, exhibitions, and conferences. The surrounding area has been transformed into a vast recreational complex, offering green spaces, playgrounds, and sports facilities for the enjoyment of locals and visitors alike. Visiting the Centennial Hall allows you to witness the convergence of architectural brilliance, historical significance, and cultural vibrancy. Its unique design, coupled with its enduring legacy as a symbol of Wroclaw's heritage, makes it a must-see destination for architecture enthusiasts, history buffs, and anyone seeking to appreciate the cultural riches of this captivating city.

Wroclaw's Dwarfs (Krasnale)

Wroclaw's Dwarfs, or "Krasnale" in Polish, are a delightful and whimsical feature that adds a touch of magic to the streets of Wroclaw. These tiny bronze statues have become an iconic symbol of the city, capturing the imagination of both locals and visitors. The story of the Wroclaw Dwarfs began in the 1980s as a form of peaceful protest against the communist regime. A group of artists known as the Orange Alternative used the dwarf as a symbol of their resistance, representing the idea that even small and seemingly insignificant beings could challenge authority. Since then, the dwarfs have taken on a life of their own and have become an integral part of Wroclaw's identity.

Today, over 600 dwarf statues can be found scattered throughout the city, hidden in plain sight. Each dwarf has its own unique character and story, often reflecting a specific occupation, historical event, or cultural reference. Some dwarfs can be found on the ground, while others may be perched on benches, walls, or even peering out from underground. Discovering the dwarfs of Wroclaw is like embarking on a whimsical treasure hunt. As you explore the city, keep your eyes peeled for these playful creatures, as they may be found in unexpected places. From the main streets and squares to hidden corners and alleys, the dwarfs have infiltrated all corners of Wroclaw, creating a sense of wonder and surprise.

Finding the dwarfs is not only a fun and interactive activity but also an opportunity to delve deeper into the city's history and culture. Each dwarf has a story to tell, often reflecting Wroclaw's heritage or commemorating significant events. From the "Pisanki" dwarf, symbolizing the tradition of decorating Easter eggs, to the "Pisarz" dwarf, representing the city's literary heritage, each statue provides a glimpse into the rich tapestry of Wroclaw's past. The dwarfs have become beloved mascots of the city, bringing joy to locals and tourists alike. They have also become a symbol of solidarity and freedom, reminding people of the power of unity and creativity in the face of adversity.

As you embark on your exploration of Wroclaw, make sure to pick up a dwarf map from one of the tourist information centers or download a mobile app that will guide you to the various dwarf locations. You can even challenge yourself to find as many dwarfs as possible and create your own adventure along the way.

Wroclaw's Dwarfs are more than just statues; they are an embodiment of the city's playful spirit, cultural heritage, and sense of community. Whether you're young or young at heart, these charming creatures are sure to put a smile on your face and create lasting memories of your visit to this enchanting city.

Panorama of the Battle of Racławice

The Panorama of the Battle of Racławice is a magnificent work of art that transports visitors back in time to a crucial moment in Polish history. Located in Wroclaw, Poland, this panoramic painting depicts the Battle of Racławice, fought during the Kościuszko Uprising in

1794, and stands as a testament to the artistic and historical significance of the event.

The panorama was created by a team of talented artists led by Jan Styka and Wojciech Kossak. It was completed in 1894, on the centenary of the battle, to commemorate the bravery and resilience of the Polish forces led by Tadeusz Kościuszko against the Russian Empire. The enormous circular painting, measuring 15 meters (49 feet) in height and 114 meters (374 feet) in circumference, provides viewers with an immersive experience as they step into the depicted scene. Entering the panorama hall, visitors are immediately enveloped by a three-dimensional representation of the battle. The cylindrical canvas surrounds them, creating the illusion of being in the midst of the action. The incredibly detailed painting captures the intensity, chaos, and heroism of the battle, portraying the Polish rebels in their struggle against the Russian forces.

As you explore the panorama, you'll notice the meticulous attention to detail. The painting showcases the diverse array of characters and scenes, from soldiers engaged in combat to civilians witnessing the conflict. The landscape, costumes, and weaponry are all meticulously rendered, allowing visitors to immerse themselves in the historical context of the battle. The panorama is not just a visual spectacle but also incorporates sound and lighting effects, enhancing the immersive experience. The carefully designed lighting creates the illusion of different times of day, enhancing the atmosphere and adding depth to the scene. Combined with the accompanying soundtrack, which includes the sounds of battle and narrations, the panorama comes to life, evoking an emotional response from viewers.

Beyond its artistic merits, the Panorama of the Battle of Racławice is an important historical artifact. It provides a glimpse into a pivotal moment in Polish history when the nation fought for independence and freedom. The battle itself was a significant victory for the Polish forces, inspiring future generations and becoming a symbol of Polish resistance against foreign powers. Visiting the

Panorama of the Battle of Racławice is a unique and powerful experience. It offers a chance to witness history come alive, to appreciate the artistry and craftsmanship involved in creating such a monumental work, and to gain a deeper understanding of Poland's struggle for independence. The panorama stands as a testament to the enduring spirit and resilience of the Polish people and serves as a reminder of the importance of preserving and commemorating historical events. It is a must-see attraction for history enthusiasts, art lovers, and anyone seeking to immerse themselves in the captivating stories that have shaped Poland's past.

Hala Stulecia (Centennial Hall)

Hala Stulecia, also known as the Centennial Hall, is a remarkable architectural gem located in Wroclaw, Poland. This UNESCO World Heritage Site holds historical and cultural significance and stands as a testament to the innovative architectural achievements of the early 20th century. The Centennial Hall was constructed between 1911 and 1913 in celebration of the centennial anniversary of the defeat of Napoleon Bonaparte in the Battle of Leipzig. Designed by Max Berg, a renowned German architect, the hall was envisioned as a multi-purpose venue that would showcase Wroclaw's industrial and cultural prowess.

The architectural design of the Centennial Hall is characterized by its pioneering use of reinforced concrete, a revolutionary material at the time. The structure features a colossal dome with a diameter of 65 meters (213 feet) and a height of 42 meters (138 feet), making it one of the largest reinforced concrete domes in the world. The dome's intricate ribbed construction adds to its architectural splendor and serves as a remarkable example of engineering ingenuity. Surrounding the hall is a circular colonnade adorned with sculptures, friezes, and decorative elements, creating a harmonious and visually captivating ensemble. The exterior facade showcases a blend of architectural styles, including Art Nouveau and historicist influences, making the Centennial Hall a unique and eclectic masterpiece.

Inside the Centennial Hall, visitors are greeted by a spacious and versatile interior. The main hall, with a seating capacity of over 7,000 people, has hosted a wide range of events, including exhibitions, trade fairs, concerts, and sporting events. The hall's acoustics are renowned for their excellence, making it a favored venue for concerts and musical performances. Adjacent to the Centennial Hall is the Pergola, an architectural structure that complements the grandeur of the main hall. The Pergola features beautifully landscaped gardens, water features, and walkways, providing a serene and picturesque setting for leisurely strolls and relaxation.

Throughout its history, the Centennial Hall has witnessed significant events and hosted renowned personalities, including political figures, artists, and musicians. It has played a crucial role in shaping the cultural and social fabric of Wroclaw, becoming a symbol of civic pride and a gathering place for both locals and visitors.

Today, the Centennial Hall continues to serve as a vibrant cultural center, hosting a diverse array of events, exhibitions, and concerts. It has also become an iconic landmark in Wroclaw, attracting architecture enthusiasts, history buffs, and those seeking to experience the grandeur of this remarkable structure. Visiting the Centennial Hall allows you to marvel at the architectural brilliance of the past while appreciating its continued relevance in the present. It is a testament to human creativity, engineering prowess, and the enduring legacy of Wroclaw's cultural heritage.

National Museum in Wroclaw

The National Museum in Wroclaw is a cultural institution that showcases the rich artistic and historical heritage of the region. Located in the heart of Wroclaw, Poland, the museum houses a diverse collection of artworks, artifacts, and exhibitions that provide insight into the history, culture, and artistic traditions of Wroclaw and its surrounding areas. The museum traces its origins back to 1947 when it was officially established as the Museum of Wroclaw. Over the years, its collection grew through acquisitions, donations, and archaeological excavations, eventually leading to its transformation into the National Museum in 1950. Today, the museum is divided into several departments, each dedicated to specific areas of art and history. The art collection of the National Museum spans various periods and genres, offering visitors a comprehensive view of Polish and European artistic traditions. The museum boasts an extensive collection of paintings, sculptures, prints, and decorative arts, with notable works from artists such as Albrecht Dürer, Peter Paul Rubens, Claude Monet, and Stanisław Wyspiański, among others. The collection encompasses a wide range of styles, from medieval and Renaissance art to modern and contemporary masterpieces.

In addition to its art collection, the National Museum in Wroclaw also features exhibits that explore the history and archaeology of the region. Visitors can delve into the rich history of Wroclaw through displays of archaeological finds, historical artifacts, and interactive exhibits. The museum provides a glimpse into the city's past, including its medieval origins, the impact of World War II, and the post-war reconstruction. The National Museum regularly hosts temporary exhibitions that showcase various themes, artists, and artistic movements. These exhibits offer a dynamic and ever-changing experience, allowing visitors to explore different aspects of art, culture, and history. The museum building itself is a historic architectural masterpiece. Located in a former palace complex, the structure exudes elegance and grandeur, providing a fitting backdrop for the artworks and exhibits within. The museum's galleries are thoughtfully designed to create a harmonious and engaging environment for visitors to explore and appreciate the collections.

Beyond its permanent and temporary exhibitions, the National Museum in Wroclaw offers educational programs, workshops, and lectures that promote a deeper understanding and appreciation of art and history. These initiatives cater to visitors of all ages and foster a sense of curiosity and exploration.

Visiting the National Museum in Wroclaw allows you to immerse yourself in the cultural tapestry of the region, to admire masterpieces from renowned artists, and to gain a deeper understanding of Wroclaw's history and heritage. It is a destination that appeals to art enthusiasts, history lovers, and those seeking to broaden their knowledge and appreciation of Polish and European culture.

Ostrów Tumski

Ostrów Tumski, also known as Cathedral Island, is a historic and enchanting district located in Wroclaw, Poland. Situated on the banks of the Oder River, it is one of the oldest parts of the city and a place of significant cultural and religious importance. Stepping onto Ostrów Tumski feels like entering a different world. The district exudes a tranquil and mystical atmosphere, with its narrow cobblestone streets, historic buildings, and peaceful courtyards. It is a place where centuries of history and spirituality converge. At the heart of Ostrów Tumski stands the magnificent Wroclaw Cathedral, also known as the Cathedral of St. John the Baptist. This Gothic masterpiece is an architectural gem that dates back to the 10th century. Its towering spires and ornate details make it a prominent landmark on the Wroclaw skyline. Inside the cathedral, visitors can explore its intricate chapels, awe-inspiring stained glass windows, and the beautifully crafted sarcophagus of St. Hedwig of Silesia. Climbing the cathedral tower rewards visitors with breathtaking views of Wroclaw and its surroundings. Wandering through the streets of Ostrów Tumski, visitors will encounter numerous historic churches, each with its own unique charm. These include the Church of St. Giles, the Holy Cross Church, and the Church of the Holy Name of Jesus. Each church has its own story to tell and showcases architectural styles ranging from Romanesque to Baroque.

Aside from its religious significance, Ostrów Tumski also offers captivating sights and hidden treasures. The picturesque bridges that connect the district to the rest of Wroclaw, such as the Tumski Bridge, offer stunning views of the Oder River and the cityscape. The peaceful gardens and courtyards tucked away in the district provide moments of serenity amidst the historical surroundings. Ostrów Tumski is not just a place frozen in the past; it is a living district that is home to numerous institutions and cultural centers. The Archdiocese Museum, located in the former Bishop's Palace, houses a collection of religious art and artifacts. The Wroclaw Theological Seminary, where future priests are trained, is also located within Ostrów Tumski. The district comes alive during religious festivals and celebrations. The annual St. John's Fair, held in June, is a lively event where locals and visitors come together to enjoy music, food, and entertainment in the shadow of the cathedral. Exploring Ostrów Tumski allows visitors to connect with the spiritual and historical roots of Wroclaw. Its serene ambiance, architectural wonders, and profound religious significance make it a must-visit destination for those seeking a deeper understanding of the city's cultural heritage. Whether it's exploring the cathedrals, strolling along the riverbank, or simply taking in the timeless beauty, a visit to Ostrów Tumski is a journey into the soul of Wroclaw.

Hidden courtyards and passages

Wroclaw is a city filled with hidden courtyards and passages, secret enclaves tucked away behind the bustling streets. These hidden gems offer a respite from the vibrant city atmosphere and provide a glimpse into the quieter, more intimate side of Wroclaw's charm. Exploring the hidden courtyards and passages of Wroclaw is like embarking on a treasure hunt. As you wander through the city's labyrinthine streets, keep an eye out for unassuming entrances or inconspicuous archways that lead to these hidden havens. Once you step inside, you'll discover a world of tranquility and discovery. These courtyards often feature beautifully preserved historic buildings with colorful facades, flower-filled balconies, and ornate details. The architecture reflects various styles, from Renaissance and Baroque to Art Nouveau and modernist influences. Each courtyard has its own unique character, providing a snapshot of Wroclaw's architectural heritage. The courtyards are not just aesthetically pleasing; they also offer delightful surprises. Many house charming cafes, cozy restaurants, boutique shops, art galleries, and craft workshops. These hidden establishments provide an opportunity to relax, indulge in delicious cuisine, or explore unique creations crafted by local artisans. Some courtyards are connected by hidden passages, narrow alleyways that wind through the cityscape, revealing unexpected nooks and crannies. These passages often lead to hidden squares or open spaces, creating a sense of discovery and wonder as you navigate through them. The passages are adorned with street art, murals, and colorful graffiti, adding to the artistic ambiance of these hidden corners. One such hidden passage worth exploring is Pasaz Niepolda, located near the Market Square. This narrow passage is adorned with vibrant street art, creating an urban art gallery that surprises and delights visitors. It is a testament to the city's vibrant art scene and creative spirit. Another hidden gem is the courtyard of Jatki, a former slaughterhouse transformed into a lively cultural space. This courtyard is now home to artistic workshops, galleries, and a popular theater, offering a vibrant hub for creative expression. Exploring the hidden courtyards and passages of Wroclaw allows you to escape the crowds and immerse yourself in the city's hidden treasures. It offers a glimpse into the daily lives of Wroclaw's residents and a chance to experience the city's rich history, architectural beauty, and artistic vibrancy from a different perspective. As you wander through the hidden courtyards and passages, take your time to soak in the atmosphere, appreciate the architectural details, and embrace the sense of serenity that comes with discovering these secret corners. Let yourself get lost in the maze of hidden treasures, and you'll uncover the soul of Wroclaw that lies beyond its well-known landmarks and bustling streets.

From the iconic landmarks that define the city's skyline to the lesser-known corners that hold hidden treasures, Wroclaw offers a rich tapestry of experiences for every visitor. Embark on a journey of discovery, and let Wroclaw's iconic landmarks and hidden gems reveal the essence of this captivating city.

Exploring Wroclaw's Neighborhoods

Exploring the neighborhoods of Wroclaw offers a deeper understanding of the city's diverse character, vibrant culture, and rich history. Each neighborhood has its own unique atmosphere, attractions, and hidden gems waiting to be discovered. Here are some of the neighborhoods worth exploring in Wroclaw:

Stare Miasto (Old Town)

Stare Miasto, or Old Town, is the historic heart of Wroclaw and one of the most captivating neighborhoods in the city. Steeped in history, this charming district showcases a remarkable blend of architectural styles, cultural attractions, and a vibrant atmosphere that draws locals and visitors alike. At the heart of Stare Miasto lies the magnificent Market Square (Rynek), one of the largest medieval squares in Europe. This bustling square is surrounded by colorful townhouses adorned with intricate facades, creating a picturesque setting. The centerpiece of the Market Square is the iconic Town

Hall, a Gothic masterpiece that stands as a symbol of Wroclaw's rich history. Visitors can climb the tower for panoramic views or explore the Wroclaw City Museum housed within its walls. Wandering through the narrow streets of Stare Miasto, you'll encounter numerous architectural gems. From Gothic churches like the Church of St. Elizabeth, with its stunning stained glass windows, to the Baroque splendor of the Holy Cross Church, each structure tells a story of the city's past. The historic architecture is beautifully preserved, creating an ambiance that transports visitors to a bygone era.

Stare Miasto is also home to vibrant cafes, restaurants, and shops. Its lively atmosphere makes it an ideal place to relax, indulge in delicious cuisine, and soak up the local culture. Sample traditional Polish dishes, enjoy a cup of aromatic coffee, or browse through boutique shops offering unique handicrafts and souvenirs. The district is not just about historic buildings; it also boasts cultural institutions and artistic spaces. The National Museum in Wroclaw houses an impressive collection of art and historical artifacts, providing insights into the region's cultural heritage. The Opera Wroclawska, located in a beautiful Neo-Baroque building, offers world-class opera and ballet performances. Stare Miasto comes alive with festivals and events throughout the year. The Christmas Market, with its festive decorations and twinkling lights, transforms the Market Square into a winter wonderland. During the Wroclaw Good Beer Festival, beer enthusiasts gather to sample a wide variety of craft beers from Poland and beyond.

Exploring Stare Miasto is not just about visiting landmarks; it's about immersing yourself in the city's vibrant spirit, connecting with its history, and embracing its lively atmosphere. The neighborhood's architectural beauty, cultural treasures, and inviting ambiance make it a must-visit destination that truly captures the essence of Wroclaw.

Nadodrze

Nadodrze is a vibrant and eclectic neighborhood in Wroclaw that is known for its artistic flair and bohemian atmosphere. Located just north of the city center, it has become a hub for creatives, alternative culture, and urban exploration. The neighborhood's name, Nadodrze, means "beyond the river," as it is situated on the left bank of the Oder River. Crossing one of the picturesque bridges from the city center leads you into this captivating district. Nadodrze is renowned for its vibrant street art scene. Walking through its streets, you'll encounter colorful and striking murals, graffiti, and art installations that adorn buildings, walls, and even entire facades. The art reflects various themes, ranging from social commentary to abstract and imaginative designs. Exploring the streets of Nadodrze is like stepping into an open-air art gallery, where every corner holds a visual surprise. The neighborhood is also home to numerous galleries, art studios, and creative spaces. Artists, designers, and craftsmen have set up shop in Nadodrze, showcasing their works and contributing to the neighborhood's vibrant artistic energy. Visiting these galleries and workshops offers a glimpse into the local art scene and provides an opportunity to engage with the creative community.

In addition to its artistic character, Nadodrze has a lively and welcoming atmosphere. The neighborhood is dotted with hip cafes, trendy bars, and unique eateries that cater to diverse tastes. You can savor artisanal coffee, enjoy craft beers, or sample international and fusion cuisines. The lively nightlife in Nadodrze offers a range of options, from cozy pubs with live music to underground clubs hosting alternative events. Nadodrze also hosts regular cultural events and festivals that celebrate its artistic spirit. The "Nadodrze Fair" showcases local craftsmanship, art, and design, offering a platform for artists and artisans to present their work to a wider audience. The neighborhood's streets come alive with music, performances, and cultural activities during these events, creating a vibrant and festive ambiance.

Beyond its artistic and culinary offerings, Nadodrze is characterized by its unique architecture and charming residential streets. Colorful tenement houses, historic facades, and hidden courtyards add to the neighborhood's charm. Exploring the quiet backstreets and hidden corners reveals a sense of nostalgia and a glimpse into the lives of its residents.

Nadodrze's bohemian atmosphere, artistic vibrancy, and sense of community make it an intriguing neighborhood to explore. It invites visitors to engage with its creativity, immerse themselves in its cultural scene, and appreciate the unique character that sets it apart from other parts of Wroclaw. Whether you're an art enthusiast, a lover of alternative culture, or simply seeking an offbeat and inspiring experience, Nadodrze is sure to captivate and leave a lasting impression.

Śródmieście

Śródmieście, which translates to "city center" in English, is a bustling and dynamic neighborhood in Wroclaw. As the commercial and administrative hub of the city, Śródmieście offers a mix of historic landmarks, modern developments, educational institutions, and a vibrant urban atmosphere. The neighborhood is anchored by the Market Square (Rynek), the heart of Wroclaw and one of the largest medieval squares in Europe. The square is surrounded by beautifully restored townhouses, cafes, restaurants, and shops. It serves as a gathering place for locals and visitors alike, with events, festivals, and outdoor markets taking place throughout the year. Śródmieście is also home to the University of Wroclaw, one of the oldest and most prestigious universities in Poland. The university's buildings, scattered throughout the neighborhood, lend an academic and youthful vibe to the area. Exploring the university campus allows you to experience the vibrant student life and appreciate the historic architecture.

Wroclaw's cultural scene thrives in Śródmieście, with numerous theaters, concert halls, and art galleries dotting the neighborhood. The Wroclaw Opera House, housed in an impressive Neo-Baroque building, hosts opera and ballet performances, captivating audiences with its world-class productions. The National Forum of Music, a modern concert hall, offers a diverse program of classical and contemporary music. Adjacent to Śródmieście is the picturesque Oder River, which provides scenic views and a beautiful waterfront promenade. Walking along the riverbank allows you to soak up the tranquil ambiance and enjoy outdoor activities, such as cycling or simply relaxing in the green spaces. The neighborhood is well-connected, with excellent public transportation links that make it easy to explore other parts of Wroclaw. The main train station, Wroclaw Główny, is located in Śródmieście, offering convenient access to regional and international destinations. Śródmieście also caters to shoppers with its diverse retail options. You'll find a mix of international brands, department stores, boutiques, and local shops. The bustling commercial streets, such as

Świdnicka and Oławska, are lined with shops offering fashion, accessories, books, and more.

When it comes to dining, Śródmieście has something for everyone. The neighborhood boasts a wide range of restaurants, cafes, and bars, catering to various tastes and budgets. From traditional Polish cuisine to international flavors, you'll find a plethora of options to satisfy your culinary cravings.

Exploring Śródmieście allows you to experience the vibrant pulse of Wroclaw. Its central location, mix of historic and contemporary landmarks, cultural institutions, and bustling streets make it a dynamic neighborhood that showcases the city's energy and diversity. Whether you're seeking history, culture, entertainment, or simply a taste of urban life, Śródmieście is a neighborhood that promises to captivate and leave a lasting impression.

Przedmieście Świdnickie

Przedmieście Świdnickie is a captivating neighborhood located just south of the Wroclaw city center. Named after the Świdnicka Gate, which used to stand at its entrance, this district offers a blend of historic charm, modern developments, and green spaces, making it a delightful place to explore. One of the highlights of Przedmieście Świdnickie is the Centennial Hall complex, a UNESCO World Heritage Site. The Centennial Hall, also known as Hala Stulecia, is an architectural masterpiece that dates back to the early 20th century. Its massive dome and intricate details showcase the innovative use of reinforced concrete. The hall hosts a variety of events, including concerts, exhibitions, and trade fairs. Surrounding the hall is the tranquil Pergola garden, with its manicured lawns, fountains, and picturesque walkways, providing a serene retreat. The neighborhood is also home to the Wroclaw Congress Center, a modern venue that hosts conferences, conventions, and cultural events. Its sleek and contemporary architecture adds to the district's overall appeal. Przedmieście Świdnickie is characterized by its blend of architectural styles. Along the historic Świdnicka Street, you'll find charming townhouses with colorful facades and ornate details. This vibrant street is lined with cafes, restaurants, and shops, offering a lively atmosphere and plenty of opportunities for indulging in local cuisine, shopping, or simply people-watching.

Adjacent to the neighborhood is the beautiful Szczytnicki Park, a vast green oasis that beckons visitors to unwind and enjoy nature. Within the park, you'll find the enchanting Japanese Garden, a serene retreat with traditional Japanese landscaping, pagodas, and ponds filled with koi fish. The Multimedia Fountain, located nearby, offers dazzling water and light shows that captivate audiences. Przedmieście Świdnickie is well-connected to the rest of Wroclaw, with convenient public transportation options. The neighborhood's proximity to the main train station, Wroclaw Główny, and its central location make it easily accessible.

The neighborhood is also known for its rich culinary scene. Along Świdnicka Street and its surrounding streets, you'll find a variety of eateries offering diverse cuisines, ranging from traditional Polish dishes to international flavors. Whether you're craving pierogi, sushi, or a hearty Polish meal, Przedmieście Świdnickie has something to satisfy your taste buds. Exploring Przedmieście Świdnickie allows you to experience the harmonious blend of history, culture, and natural beauty. From architectural marvels to lush green spaces, this neighborhood offers a little something for everyone. Whether you're interested in history, seeking relaxation in the park, or looking for a vibrant culinary experience, Przedmieście Świdnickie is a neighborhood that invites you to immerse yourself in its unique charm and embrace the best of what Wroclaw has to offer.

Sępolno

Sępolno is a tranquil and picturesque neighborhood located on the outskirts of Wroclaw, Poland. Situated to the east of the city center, this residential area offers a peaceful retreat from the bustling urban environment. The neighborhood is known for its green spaces and natural beauty. It is home to the sprawling Szczytnicki Park, a vast expanse of greenery that provides a serene escape from the city. The park is ideal for leisurely walks, jogging, or simply relaxing amidst nature. Within Szczytnicki Park, you'll find the enchanting Japanese Garden, a meticulously designed oasis featuring traditional Japanese landscaping, serene ponds, pagodas, and stone lanterns. It offers a tranquil setting for contemplation and appreciation of nature's beauty. Sępolno is also where you'll find the Wroclaw Zoological Garden, one of the oldest and largest zoos in Poland. Spanning over 33 hectares, the zoo is home to a diverse range of animal species from around the world. Visitors can explore various exhibits, watch feeding sessions, and learn about wildlife conservation efforts. The zoo provides a fun and educational experience for visitors of all ages.

Aside from its natural attractions, Sępolno offers a sense of community and a residential charm. The neighborhood features a mix of architectural styles, including modern developments and charming houses with well-tended gardens. It provides a peaceful setting for families, retirees, and anyone seeking a quieter residential environment. Sępolno is also well-connected to the rest of Wroclaw. The neighborhood is served by public transportation, making it easy to reach other parts of the city. Additionally, its proximity to major roads and highways allows for convenient access to neighboring towns and attractions.

Exploring Sępolno provides an opportunity to appreciate the beauty of Wroclaw's natural landscapes and immerse oneself in a peaceful and residential atmosphere. Whether you're visiting the zoo, strolling through Szczytnicki Park, or simply enjoying the tranquility of the neighborhood, Sępolno offers a refreshing contrast to the city center and allows you to connect with nature and unwind in a serene environment.

Krzyki

Krzyki is a vibrant and diverse neighborhood located in the southern part of Wroclaw, Poland. Known for its residential charm, green spaces, and lively atmosphere, Krzyki offers a unique blend of tranquility and urban energy. The neighborhood is characterized by its picturesque streets lined with colorful townhouses, charming parks, and tree-lined boulevards. Walking through Krzyki, you'll notice the neighborhood's relaxed and inviting ambiance. It is a place where locals take leisurely strolls, children play in the parks, and residents enjoy the community spirit. Krzyki is renowned for its numerous community parks and green spaces. Park Południowy, one of the largest parks in Wroclaw, provides ample opportunities for outdoor activities such as jogging, cycling, and picnicking. With its sprawling lawns, tree-lined paths, and tranquil ponds, the park offers a serene retreat where residents can unwind and enjoy nature. Another notable park in Krzyki is Park Kleciński, a picturesque oasis with scenic walking trails, a charming pond, and a forested area. It is an ideal place to escape the city hustle and bustle and reconnect with nature. The neighborhood also boasts a vibrant food scene with a wide range of culinary options. From traditional Polish cuisine to international flavors, you'll find numerous restaurants, cafes, and bars offering diverse menus. Whether you're in the mood for a hearty Polish meal, a gourmet burger, or a taste of international cuisine, Krzyki has something to satisfy every palate.

Krzyki is also home to a thriving local market scene. The Hala Targowa market, situated in the neighborhood, offers a variety of fresh produce, artisanal products, and local delicacies. It is a great place to experience the lively atmosphere, interact with vendors, and discover the flavors of Wroclaw. The neighborhood's vibrant energy extends to its cultural offerings as well. The Capitol Musical Theatre, located in Krzyki, hosts a range of performances, including musicals, concerts, and theatrical productions. It is a popular venue that attracts locals and visitors with its diverse program of entertainment. Krzyki's excellent transportation links make it easily accessible from other parts of Wroclaw. The neighborhood is well-served by public transportation, including tram and bus lines, ensuring convenient connectivity throughout the city. Exploring Krzyki allows you to experience the residential charm, green spaces, and local community spirit that define the neighborhood. Whether you're strolling through the parks, sampling local cuisine, or enjoying cultural performances, Krzyki offers a vibrant and welcoming environment that showcases the best of Wroclaw's diverse and dynamic character.

Exploring Wroclaw's neighborhoods allows you to experience the city's diverse facets, from its historic charm to its artistic vibrancy and local communities. Each neighborhood has its own distinct character, offering a unique perspective on the city's culture, history, and lifestyle. So venture beyond the main tourist areas and discover the hidden treasures that await in Wroclaw's neighborhoods.

Things you should know before traveling to Wroclaw

Before traveling to Wroclaw, it's important to gather some essential information to ensure a smooth and enjoyable trip. This vibrant city in Poland offers a rich historical and cultural experience, but knowing a few key details beforehand will help you make the most of your visit. From practical tips to cultural insights, here are some things you should know before traveling to Wroclaw.

Currency and Language

Currency

The official currency of Poland is the Polish złoty (PLN). When traveling to Wroclaw, it's advisable to have some local currency on hand for small purchases and transactions. While credit cards are widely accepted in most hotels, restaurants, and larger establishments, it's always a good idea to carry some cash for smaller shops, markets, and local vendors. ATMs are widely available throughout the city, allowing you to withdraw złoty using your debit or credit card. Here are some important details about currency in Wroclaw to help you navigate your financial transactions during your visit:

- **Currency Exchange:** Currency exchange services are widely available in Wroclaw, particularly in tourist areas, airports, train stations, and major shopping centers. Banks, exchange offices (kantor), and some hotels provide currency exchange services. It's advisable to compare exchange rates and fees to ensure you get the best value for your money. Be cautious when exchanging currency with street vendors or unofficial exchange services, as they may offer unfavorable rates or engage in scams.

- **ATM Withdrawals:** ATMs, known as bankomats, are readily available throughout Wroclaw. They accept most major international debit and credit cards, including Visa and Mastercard. ATMs offer a convenient way to withdraw cash in the local currency. Keep in mind that your home bank may charge fees for international withdrawals, so it's advisable to check with your bank before traveling.

- **Credit Cards:** Credit cards are widely accepted in Wroclaw, particularly in hotels, upscale restaurants, and larger establishments. Visa and Mastercard are the most commonly accepted cards, followed by American Express and Diners Club, although acceptance may vary. It's a good idea to inform your credit card company or bank of your travel plans to avoid any issues with card usage abroad. Some smaller shops, markets, or local vendors may only accept cash, so it's a good idea to have some złoty on hand.

- **Tipping:** Tipping is not obligatory in Poland, but it is customary to leave a small gratuity for good service. In restaurants, it's common to round up the bill or leave a 10% tip if you are satisfied with the service. Some restaurants may include a service charge (service fee) in the bill, so it's worth checking before adding an additional tip. In bars, cafes, and taxis, it's common to round up the amount to the nearest złoty or leave a small amount as a tip for good service.

- **Payment Options:** Cash is widely accepted throughout Wroclaw, especially in smaller establishments, local markets, and for street vendors. However, many businesses, hotels, and restaurants also accept credit cards, so you can choose your preferred payment method based on your convenience and the establishment's policy. Contactless payments, using cards or mobile payment options, are becoming increasingly popular and widely accepted in Wroclaw.

By being aware of the currency and payment options in Wroclaw, you can ensure a smooth and hassle-free financial experience during your visit. It's always advisable to carry a mix of cash and cards, notify your bank of your travel plans, and exercise caution when exchanging currency or using ATMs.

Language

The official language of Wroclaw and Poland is Polish. While Polish is the primary language spoken by locals, you'll find that many people, especially those working in the tourism industry, speak English. In popular tourist areas, hotels, restaurants, and shops, you'll have no trouble communicating in English. However, it's always appreciated when visitors make an effort to learn a few basic Polish phrases. Simple greetings such as "Dzień dobry" (Good day), "Dziękuję" (Thank you), and "Proszę" (Please) can go a long way in showing respect and engaging with the local culture. If you plan to venture outside the main tourist areas, especially in more rural parts of Poland, you may encounter fewer English speakers. In such cases, having a pocket-sized phrasebook or a translation app on your phone can be useful for basic communication. Learning a few key phrases in the local language can also enhance your travel experience and make interactions with locals more enjoyable. The Polish people are generally friendly and appreciate the effort when visitors try to speak a few words in their language. Here are some key points about the language to help you communicate effectively during your visit:

- **English Proficiency:** English is widely spoken in Wroclaw, especially in popular tourist areas, hotels, restaurants, and larger establishments. You will generally have no trouble finding English-speaking staff who can assist you with your needs. Many younger people, particularly those in the service industry, have a good command of English.

- **Basic Polish Phrases:** While English is prevalent, making an effort to learn a few basic Polish phrases can go a long way in showing respect and engaging with the local culture. Locals appreciate when visitors make an effort to communicate in their language. Here are a few common Polish phrases to get you started:

- *Dzień dobry: Good day (used for greetings)*
- *Proszę: Please/You're welcome*
- *Dziękuję: Thank you*
- *Przepraszam: Excuse me/I'm sorry*
- *Czy mówisz po angielsku?: Do you speak English?*

- **Language Apps and Translation Tools:** If you want to delve deeper into the Polish language or require more complex translations, language apps and translation tools can be helpful. There are several smartphone apps available that offer basic language lessons, translations, and pronunciation guides. These can assist you in understanding menus, signs, and basic interactions.

- **Signage and Information:** In tourist areas, you will find that signs, maps, and other informational materials are often available in English as well as Polish. This makes it easier for visitors to navigate the city and find important information. Additionally, staff at tourist information centers can provide guidance and assistance in English.

- **Cultural Sensitivity:** Polish people appreciate visitors who show an interest in their culture and language. Making an effort to learn a few basic phrases and greeting locals with a polite "Dzień dobry" or "Cześć" (Hello) can go a long way in establishing a positive connection. It's important to remember that cultural customs and etiquette may vary, so be open-minded and respectful of local traditions and practices.

While Polish is the primary language in Wroclaw, English is widely spoken, making communication relatively easy for visitors. By learning a few basic phrases and embracing the local language and culture, you can enhance your travel experience and foster connections with the friendly locals of Wroclaw.

Getting Around

Wroclaw has a well-developed public transportation system, including trams and buses, making it easy to navigate the city. Consider purchasing a travel card or multiple-use tickets for convenient and cost-effective transportation. The city is also very walkable, with many attractions located within close proximity to each other. Here are some key details about getting around in Wroclaw:

- **Public Transportation:** Wroclaw has an efficient and extensive public transportation system, including trams and buses. Trams are a popular mode of transport and cover most areas of the city. They are known for their reliability and frequency. Buses complement the tram network and provide additional coverage, including to suburban areas. Tickets can be purchased from vending machines at tram stops or directly from the driver when boarding the bus. It's important to validate your ticket upon boarding the tram or bus.

- **Tickets and Passes:** Wroclaw's public transportation system operates on a zone-based ticketing system. Single-use tickets are valid for a specific time duration within designated zones. If you plan to use public transport extensively, it's recommended to consider purchasing a travel card or multiple-use tickets, such as a 24-hour or 72-hour pass, which offer unlimited travel within a specified time period. These passes can be more cost-effective for frequent travelers.

- **Tram and Bus Schedules:** Trams and buses in Wroclaw generally operate from early morning until late at night. While the frequency varies depending on the line and time of day, trams and buses typically run every 10-15 minutes during peak hours and every 20-30 minutes during off-peak hours. It's advisable to check the schedules and plan your trips accordingly, especially if you are traveling during weekends or public holidays when services may be less frequent.

- **Taxis:** Taxis are readily available in Wroclaw, and they offer a convenient mode of transportation, especially for shorter distances or when traveling with luggage. It's recommended to use licensed taxis that display a company logo and have a meter. Taxis can be hailed on the street or booked through taxi apps. Be aware that fares may vary depending on the time of day and the distance traveled. It's customary to tip taxi drivers by rounding up the fare or adding a small gratuity.

- **Walking and Cycling:** Wroclaw is a pedestrian-friendly city, and many of its attractions are within walking distance of each other, particularly in the city center. Walking allows you to soak in the charming atmosphere and discover hidden gems along the way. Cycling is also a popular option, and the city provides designated bike lanes and bike-sharing services, making it easy to explore on two wheels. You can rent bikes from various bike rental stations throughout the city.

- **Parking:** If you plan to drive in Wroclaw, it's important to familiarize yourself with parking regulations. The city has both paid parking zones and free parking areas. Paid parking zones are typically indicated by blue markings on the pavement, and payment can be made at parking meters or through mobile parking apps. Free parking areas are available in some parts of the city but may require longer walks to reach central attractions.

By utilizing Wroclaw's efficient public transportation system, walking, or cycling, you can easily navigate the city and reach its various attractions. Whether you prefer the convenience of trams and buses or enjoy exploring on foot, Wroclaw offers transportation options that cater to different preferences and make it convenient to explore the city and its surroundings.

Safety and Security

Wroclaw is generally a safe city for travelers, but like any destination, it's important to take standard precautions. Keep an eye on your belongings, avoid displaying expensive items, and be cautious in crowded places. As with any city, it's advisable to stay informed about local regulations and follow any safety advisories. Here are some key tips to ensure a safe and secure visit to Wroclaw:

- **Awareness and Vigilance:** Maintain a general level of awareness of your surroundings, especially in crowded areas and tourist spots. Keep an eye on your belongings and be cautious of pickpockets, particularly in crowded places like public transportation, markets, and tourist attractions. Avoid displaying valuable items and be mindful of your personal belongings, such as bags, wallets, and cameras.

- **Emergency Numbers:** Make note of the local emergency numbers in Wroclaw, including 112 for general emergencies. This number can be used to contact police, ambulance, or fire services. It's advisable to have a working mobile phone with you at all times in case of emergencies.

- **Travel Insurance:** Before traveling to Wroclaw or any destination, it's recommended to have comprehensive travel insurance that covers medical emergencies, trip cancellations, and loss or theft of belongings. Ensure that your insurance policy provides adequate coverage for your specific needs and activities during your trip.

- **Health and Medical Facilities:** Wroclaw has a well-developed healthcare system with hospitals, clinics, and pharmacies. If you require medical assistance, look for the nearest medical facility or contact the local emergency services. It's advisable to have travel insurance that covers medical expenses and to carry any necessary medication or prescriptions with you.

- **Local Laws and Customs:** Familiarize yourself with the local laws and customs of Poland to ensure you have a respectful and trouble-free visit. Observe local regulations, such as traffic rules, and be mindful of any specific cultural or religious practices. It's important to respect the customs and traditions of the local population.

- **Solo Travel and Nighttime Safety:** Wroclaw is generally safe for solo travelers, but it's advisable to take precautions when traveling alone, especially at night. Stick to well-lit and populated areas, and avoid walking alone in poorly lit or deserted streets. If you plan to be out late, consider using reputable taxi services or public transportation to ensure a safe return to your accommodation.

- **Emergency Preparedness:** Before your trip, familiarize yourself with the location of your embassy or consulate in Wroclaw and register with them if necessary. Keep a photocopy of your important travel documents, such as your passport and visa, in a safe place separate from the originals. It's also advisable to share your travel itinerary with a trusted friend or family member.

While Wroclaw is generally safe, it's always important to use common sense, exercise caution, and be aware of your surroundings. By following these safety tips, you can enjoy a secure and worry-free visit to Wroclaw and fully immerse yourself in the city's rich culture and attractions.

Local Customs and Etiquette

Polish people are known for their warm hospitality, and a few cultural insights can help enhance your interactions. It's customary to greet locals with a polite "Dzień dobry" (Good day) or "Cześć" (Hello). When entering churches or religious sites, dress modestly and observe any rules or customs. Tipping in restaurants and for services is appreciated, typically rounding up the bill or leaving a 10% gratuity. Here are some key points to keep in mind:

- **Greetings:** Polish people appreciate polite greetings. When meeting someone, it is customary to say "Dzień dobry" (Good day) or "Cześć" (Hello). Handshakes are a common form of greeting, especially in formal situations. Close friends or family members may greet each other with a kiss on the cheek.

- **Punctuality:** Punctuality is generally valued in Polish culture. It's considered polite to arrive on time for appointments, meetings, and social gatherings. If you anticipate being late, it's polite to inform the other party in advance.

- **Table Manners:** When dining with others, it's customary to wait until everyone is seated before starting the meal. It's polite to keep your hands visible on the table and not place them in your lap. It's also customary to say "Smacznego" (Enjoy your meal) before starting to eat. When finished, place your utensils parallel to each other on the plate to indicate that you have finished eating.

- **Politeness and Respect:** Polish people appreciate politeness and respect in interactions. Addressing people using their titles and surnames, such as "Pani" (Mrs.) or "Pan" (Mr.), is a sign of respect, particularly in formal situations. Use "Proszę" (Please) and "Dziękuję" (Thank you) frequently to show appreciation.

- **Dress Code:** Wroclaw is a modern and cosmopolitan city, and the dress code is generally casual and relaxed. However, when visiting religious sites or attending formal events, it's advisable to dress modestly. In churches, it's respectful to cover shoulders and avoid wearing revealing clothing.

- **Gift Giving:** If invited to someone's home, it's customary to bring a small gift for the host as a token of appreciation. Flowers, chocolates, or a bottle of wine are common choices. When presenting the gift, it's polite to offer it with both hands.

- **Tipping:** Tipping in Wroclaw is not obligatory but is appreciated for good service. In restaurants, it's common to leave a small gratuity by rounding up the bill or adding a 10% tip. Some restaurants may include a service charge (service fee) in the bill, so it's worth checking before adding an additional tip.

Tipping taxi drivers and hotel staff is also customary.

- **Religion and Traditions:** Poland is predominantly Catholic, and religious customs are respected and observed. When entering churches or religious sites, it's important to dress modestly and behave respectfully. During religious ceremonies, it's customary to maintain silence and avoid using flash photography.

By respecting local customs and following these etiquette guidelines, you can show appreciation for Polish culture and foster positive interactions with the locals in Wroclaw. Embracing local traditions and demonstrating polite behavior will enhance your experience and create a memorable visit to the city.

Opening Hours

Wroclaw has a diverse range of attractions, shops, and restaurants, each with its own operating hours. Many museums and cultural sites are closed on Mondays or have limited hours on specific days, so it's advisable to check their schedules in advance. Shops and supermarkets generally operate from early morning until late evening, with some closures on Sundays.

- **Shops and Retail Stores:** Most shops in Wroclaw operate during regular business hours, which are typically from Monday to Friday, between 9:00 AM and 6:00 PM. Some larger shopping centers and malls may have extended hours, staying open until 8:00 PM or later. On Saturdays, shops usually close earlier, around 3:00 PM or 4:00 PM, while on Sundays, many stores are closed or have limited hours. However, exceptions can be found, especially in tourist areas, where some shops may remain open on Sundays.

- **Supermarkets and Convenience Stores:** Supermarkets in Wroclaw generally have longer opening hours compared to other retail stores. Many are open seven days a week and operate from early morning until late evening, often until 10:00 PM or even midnight. Some smaller convenience stores or neighborhood shops may have more limited hours, but you can still find essential items outside regular business hours.

- **Museums and Cultural Institutions:** Museum and gallery opening hours in Wroclaw can vary. Most museums are closed on Mondays, and some may have additional closure days during the week. The operating hours are typically from Tuesday to Sunday, between 10:00 AM and 6:00 PM. It's recommended to check the specific museum's website or contact them in advance to confirm their opening days and hours, as they may have special exhibitions or events that could affect their schedule.

- **Restaurants and Cafes:** Wroclaw's dining scene offers a wide range of options, and opening hours for restaurants and cafes can vary. Many restaurants open for lunch around noon and serve until late evening. It's common for restaurants to take a break between lunch and dinner service, so some may be closed during the afternoon. Cafes and coffee shops often open earlier, serving breakfast and coffee from the early morning hours. Some cafes may stay open late into the evening, providing a cozy spot for socializing or enjoying a drink.

- **Bars and Nightlife:** Wroclaw has a vibrant nightlife scene, with numerous bars, pubs, and clubs to choose from. Bars generally start to get busy in the evening, with some staying open until the early morning hours. Nightclubs often open later, around 10:00 PM or later, and stay open until the early hours of the morning, particularly on weekends. The closing hours of bars and clubs can vary, so it's advisable to check their specific opening times or inquire locally for up-to-date information.

It's important to note that opening hours can be subject to change, especially during public holidays, special events, or unforeseen circumstances. It's always a good idea to check the opening hours of specific establishments, attractions, or museums before your visit, either through their websites, social media channels, or by contacting them directly. This will help you plan your itinerary effectively and ensure that you don't miss out on any experiences during your time in Wroclaw.

Sightseeing and Cultural Experiences

Wroclaw is a city teeming with history, culture, and architectural splendor. Don't miss the Market Square (Rynek), the heart of the city, and its impressive Gothic Town Hall. Explore the historic Ostrów Tumski, visit the stunning Wroclaw Cathedral, and marvel at the architectural marvel of the Centennial Hall. Immerse yourself in the local culture by trying traditional Polish cuisine, attending cultural events, and exploring the vibrant street art scene. Here are some highlights to consider:

- **Market Square (Rynek):** Start your exploration in the heart of Wroclaw at the Market Square, one of the largest medieval squares in Europe. Admire the colorful facades of the beautifully restored townhouses, enjoy a meal at one of the outdoor cafes, and soak in the lively atmosphere of this bustling square. Don't forget to visit the Gothic-style Town Hall and its astronomical clock.

- **Ostrów Tumski (Cathedral Island):** Explore the historic Ostrów Tumski, also known as Cathedral Island. This atmospheric district is home to the magnificent Wroclaw Cathedral and other historic churches. Stroll along the cobblestone streets, visit the religious sites, and witness the stunning views of the city from the bridges that connect the island to the rest of Wroclaw.

- **Centennial Hall (Hala Stulecia):** Marvel at the architectural masterpiece of Centennial Hall, a UNESCO World Heritage Site. Designed by Max Berg, this early 20th-century structure showcases innovative engineering and hosts various cultural events, exhibitions, and concerts. Explore the surrounding park and enjoy the tranquil atmosphere.

- **Museums and Galleries:** Wroclaw boasts a range of museums and galleries that cater to various interests. The National Museum in Wroclaw houses a vast collection of art, including Polish and European masterpieces. The Panorama of the Battle of Racławice offers a unique immersive experience, showcasing a monumental 19th-century panoramic painting. The Museum of Architecture showcases the city's architectural heritage, while the Wroclaw Contemporary Museum focuses on modern and contemporary art.

- **Events and Festivals:** Wroclaw hosts numerous cultural events and festivals throughout the year. The Wroclaw Christmas Market, held in the Market Square during the holiday season, is a magical experience with its festive atmosphere, crafts, and traditional treats. The Wroclaw Good Beer Festival celebrates the city's brewing traditions, offering a chance to sample local beers. Other notable events include the International Festival of Puppet Theater, Wroclaw Jazz Festival, and Wroclaw Music Night.

- **University Life:** Immerse yourself in the vibrant university culture of Wroclaw by exploring the University Quarter. Visit the stunning main building of the University of Wroclaw, known as the University's Leopoldinum, and stroll through the picturesque campus. The university area also offers a lively atmosphere with student-friendly cafes, bookstores, and cultural venues.

- **Wroclaw Dwarfs (Krasnale):** Discover the whimsical Wroclaw Dwarfs scattered throughout the city. These small bronze statues are hidden in various locations, representing different professions, hobbies, and historical events. Hunting for the dwarfs adds a fun and unique element to your sightseeing experience, allowing you to explore different parts of the city.

These are just a few of the many sightseeing and cultural experiences that await you in Wroclaw. Whether you're interested in history, art, architecture, or vibrant festivals, Wroclaw offers a rich tapestry of experiences that will leave you with lasting memories of this enchanting city.

By familiarizing yourself with these essential details before your trip to Wroclaw, you'll be better prepared to navigate the city, engage with the local culture, and make the most of your visit. Wroclaw's unique blend of history, culture, and warm hospitality promises a memorable and enriching travel experience.

Dos and Don'ts in Wroclaw

When visiting Wroclaw, it's important to be aware of the local customs and etiquette to ensure a respectful and enjoyable experience. Knowing the dos and don'ts will help you navigate the city with ease and show respect for the local culture. Here are some guidelines to keep in mind during your visit to Wroclaw.

Dos in Wroclaw

When visiting Wroclaw, the beautiful city in Poland, it's important to be aware of the local customs and cultural norms to ensure a pleasant and respectful experience. By familiarizing yourself with the dos, you can engage with the local culture, interact with the friendly residents, and make the most of your time in Wroclaw. Here are some essential dos to keep in mind during your visit.

❖ Do greet people warmly

When visiting Wroclaw, greeting people warmly is an important aspect of Polish culture and reflects the friendly and welcoming nature of the locals. Here are some additional details on how to greet people warmly in Wroclaw:

- **Use appropriate greetings:** The most common greetings in Wroclaw and Poland are "Dzień dobry" (Good day) and "Cześć" (Hello). These greetings can be used in various contexts, such as when entering a shop, restaurant, or engaging in conversations with locals. Starting your interactions with a friendly greeting sets a positive tone and demonstrates respect for the local customs.

- **Smile and make eye contact:** Along with verbal greetings, it's important to accompany them with a warm smile and make eye contact. This non-verbal communication conveys sincerity and openness, making the interaction more pleasant and friendly.

- **Handshakes:** Handshakes are commonly used in formal or professional settings, such as when meeting someone for the first time or during business interactions. When shaking hands, offer a firm and confident grip while maintaining eye contact. It's customary to shake hands with both men and women.

- **Follow social cues:** In informal settings or among friends and acquaintances, you may encounter more relaxed greetings, such as hugs or kisses on the cheek. Follow the lead of the locals in these situations. If someone extends their hand for a handshake, reciprocate accordingly. If someone leans in for a hug or kiss, feel free to respond in kind.

- **Use titles and surnames:** When meeting someone for the first time or in more formal situations, it's polite to use titles and surnames as a sign of respect. Address someone as "Pan" (Mr.) or "Pani"

(Mrs.) followed by their last name. For example, "Pan Kowalski" or "Pani Nowak". As you establish a closer relationship or if the person invites you to use their first name, you can shift to a more familiar form of address.

- **Return greetings:** If someone greets you, it's important to respond in kind. Return the greeting with a smile and a reciprocal greeting. For example, if someone says "Dzień dobry", respond with "Dzień dobry" or "Cześć". This simple gesture acknowledges the person and fosters a positive atmosphere.

By greeting people warmly in Wroclaw, you show respect for the local culture and create a friendly environment for interactions. The locals appreciate the effort made to engage in a warm and polite manner, which can lead to more meaningful connections and enrich your overall experience in the city.

❖ Do embrace the local cuisine

Embracing the local cuisine is an essential part of experiencing Wroclaw's vibrant culinary culture. Polish cuisine is known for its hearty and flavorful dishes, and trying the local food will introduce you to the authentic flavors and traditions of the region. Here are some additional details on how to embrace the local cuisine in Wroclaw:

- **Try traditional Polish dishes:** Polish cuisine is diverse and offers a range of delicious dishes. Don't miss the opportunity to savor classic Polish favorites like pierogi (dumplings) filled with various ingredients such as meat, cheese, mushrooms, or fruit. Other must-try dishes include żurek (sour rye soup), bigos (hunter's stew), and kielbasa (sausages). These dishes showcase the rich flavors and culinary heritage of Poland.

- **Explore local markets and food stalls:** Wroclaw boasts vibrant markets like Hala Targowa and Hala Stulecia, where you can find fresh produce, regional specialties, and local delicacies. Take a stroll through these markets to experience the bustling atmosphere and discover artisanal products, cheeses, bread, and pastries. Try regional delights like oscypek (smoked cheese) or pick up some fresh fruits to enjoy during your exploration of the city.

- **Visit traditional Polish restaurants:** Wroclaw has numerous restaurants that specialize in traditional Polish cuisine. Look for restaurants that serve authentic Polish dishes made from locally sourced ingredients. These establishments often offer a cozy and nostalgic ambiance that reflects the warmth of Polish hospitality. Ask locals or check online reviews for recommendations to find the best places to enjoy Polish cuisine in Wroclaw.

- **Attend food festivals and events:** Wroclaw hosts various food festivals and events throughout the year, providing opportunities to sample a wide range of local and international dishes. Events like the Wroclaw Good Beer Festival, Pierogi Festival, or Food Truck Festivals showcase the diverse culinary offerings in the city. Attend these festivals to taste different flavors, interact with local vendors, and immerse yourself in the food culture of Wroclaw.

- **Learn to cook Polish dishes:** For a deeper immersion into the local cuisine, consider taking a cooking class or participating in a culinary workshop. Many cooking schools in Wroclaw offer classes that teach you how to prepare traditional Polish dishes. Learn the techniques, ingredients, and flavors of Polish cooking and bring a piece of Wroclaw's culinary heritage back home with you.

- **Engage with locals for recommendations:** The best way to discover hidden culinary gems in Wroclaw is to engage with the locals. Strike up conversations with residents, ask for recommendations, and seek their insights into the city's food scene. Locals are often eager to share their favorite eateries, street food stalls, and hidden restaurants that may not be as well-known to tourists.

By embracing the local cuisine in Wroclaw, you'll not only delight your taste buds but also gain a deeper appreciation for the cultural traditions and culinary heritage of the city. Enjoy the flavors, explore the diverse offerings, and immerse yourself in the culinary delights that Wroclaw has to offer.

❖ **Do dress appropriately**

Wroclaw has a diverse mix of styles, ranging from casual to formal. When visiting religious sites, it's advisable to dress modestly and avoid wearing revealing clothing. In general, it's always a good idea to dress neatly and blend in with the local fashion. Here are some additional details on how to dress appropriately in Wroclaw:

- **Respectful attire for religious sites:** If you plan to visit churches or other religious sites in Wroclaw, it's important to dress modestly. Both men and women should avoid wearing revealing clothing, such as short skirts, shorts, or sleeveless tops. It's recommended to cover your shoulders and knees, and opt for clothing that is more conservative and respectful.

- **Casual and comfortable attire for everyday activities:** Wroclaw is a modern and cosmopolitan city, and casual attire is generally acceptable for most everyday activities. Dress comfortably for walking and exploring the city, especially during the warmer months. Choose lightweight and breathable clothing, such as t-shirts, blouses, jeans, or shorts, depending on the weather. Comfortable footwear is also essential for exploring the cobblestone streets of the city.

- **Smart casual for dining out and formal occasions:** When dining at restaurants or attending more formal events in Wroclaw, it's recommended to dress in smart casual attire. Men can opt for collared shirts, trousers, and closed-toe shoes, while women can choose dresses, skirts, or dress pants paired with blouses or tops. It's always better to be slightly overdressed than underdressed for such occasions.

- **Check dress codes for specific venues:** Some upscale restaurants, clubs, or cultural venues in Wroclaw may have specific dress codes. If you plan to visit such places, it's advisable to check their requirements in advance. Some venues may require more formal attire, such as jackets or cocktail dresses, especially in the evenings.

- **Consider the weather and season:** Wroclaw experiences different seasons, with varying temperatures throughout the year. Check the weather forecast before your visit and pack accordingly. In colder months, layering is recommended, and it's advisable to bring a warm coat, hat, and gloves. During the summer, light and breathable clothing is suitable to cope with the warmer temperatures.

- **Cultural events and performances:** If you plan to attend cultural events, such as concerts, theater performances, or operas, it's advisable to dress slightly more formal. Opt for business casual or semi-formal attire, such as dresses or dress shirts paired with trousers or skirts. It's always a good idea to check the specific dress code for the event or venue you will be attending.

Remember that dressing appropriately not only shows respect for the local culture but also enhances your overall experience in Wroclaw. By dressing modestly and comfortably, you can blend in with the locals and ensure that you're prepared for various activities and venues in the city.

❖ Do embrace public transportation

Wroclaw has a well-developed public transportation system, including trams and buses, which provides convenient and cost-effective options for getting around the city. Embrace the local transport and explore the different districts of Wroclaw, immersing yourself in the everyday life of the city. Here are some additional details on why you should embrace public transportation in Wroclaw:

- **Extensive network:** Wroclaw has a well-developed public transportation network that includes trams and buses. The network covers the entire city and connects even the more remote neighborhoods, making it easy to reach popular tourist destinations as well as off-the-beaten-path locations.

- **Cost-effective:** Public transportation in Wroclaw is relatively affordable compared to other modes of transportation. You can purchase single-ride tickets, day passes, or longer-term passes depending on the duration of your stay. Opting for public transportation can save you money on transportation expenses, especially if you plan to move around frequently.

- **Convenience and frequency:** Trams and buses in Wroclaw run regularly and adhere to fixed schedules. They offer frequent services, especially during peak hours, ensuring that you don't have to wait long for your transportation to arrive. This convenience allows you to plan your activities and explore the city efficiently.

- **Accessibility:** Wroclaw's public transportation system is designed to be accessible for everyone, including individuals with disabilities or mobility challenges. Many trams and buses are equipped with ramps or lifts, making it easier for wheelchair users or those with strollers to board and disembark.

- **Environmentally friendly:** Opting for public transportation in Wroclaw contributes to reducing carbon emissions and helps preserve the environment. Using trams and buses instead of private cars helps alleviate traffic congestion, reduce pollution, and promote sustainable transportation practices.

- **Insight into local life:** By using public transportation, you can gain a glimpse into the everyday lives of Wroclaw's residents. You'll have the opportunity to observe local customs, interact with fellow passengers, and experience the city from a different perspective. It's a chance to immerse yourself in the local culture and feel like a part of the community.

- **Convenience for day trips:** Wroclaw's public transportation system also facilitates day trips to nearby attractions and towns. You can easily access destinations like Ksiaz Castle, Swidnica with its famous Church of Peace, or other nearby cities like Poznan or Krakow, using the convenient train or bus connections from Wroclaw.

To make the most of your public transportation experience in Wroclaw, familiarize yourself with the routes, schedules, and ticketing options. Timetable information is available at tram and bus stops, and you can also use mobile apps or online resources for real-time updates. Public transportation is a reliable and practical way to get around Wroclaw, allowing you to explore the city efficiently while enjoying the benefits of convenience and cost-effectiveness.

❖ Do engage with the local culture

Engaging with the local culture in Wroclaw is a fantastic way to immerse yourself in the vibrant traditions, customs, and daily life of the city. By embracing the local culture, you can gain a deeper understanding of Wroclaw's rich heritage and create meaningful connections with its residents. Here are some additional details on how to engage with the local culture in Wroclaw:

- **Attend cultural events and festivals:** Wroclaw is known for its lively cultural scene, with a variety of events and festivals throughout the year. From music concerts and theater performances to art exhibitions and film festivals, there's always something happening in Wroclaw. Check the city's event calendar and attend local cultural events to experience the artistic talents and creative expressions of the city's residents.

- **Explore museums and galleries:** Wroclaw is home to numerous museums and galleries that showcase the city's history, art, and cultural heritage. Visit the National Museum in Wroclaw to admire the extensive collection of Polish and European artworks. Explore the Museum of Architecture to learn about Wroclaw's architectural evolution, or immerse yourself in contemporary art at the Wroclaw Contemporary Museum. These institutions offer insights into the city's cultural identity and artistic achievements.

- **Discover traditional crafts and artisanal products:** Wroclaw is known for its rich craftsmanship and traditional handicrafts. Explore local markets, artisan shops, and craft fairs to discover unique items made by local artisans. Look for traditional ceramics, handwoven textiles, woodcarvings, and other crafts that represent Wroclaw's cultural heritage. Engage with the artisans, learn about their techniques, and support the local craftsmanship.

- **Sample local cuisine:** Embracing the local cuisine is not only a delightful culinary experience but also an opportunity to engage with the local culture. Visit local restaurants, food stalls, and markets to try traditional Polish dishes and regional specialties. Engage with the chefs and food vendors, ask about the ingredients and preparation methods, and learn about the cultural significance of the dishes. Food can provide a window into the traditions, history, and local customs of a place.

- **Learn basic Polish phrases:** While many people in Wroclaw speak English, making an effort to learn a few basic Polish phrases can enhance your interactions and show respect for the local language. Greet people with a friendly "Dzień dobry" (Good day) or "Cześć" (Hello), and learn simple expressions like "Proszę" (Please) and

"Dziękuję" (Thank you). Locals will appreciate your efforts and may be more open to sharing insights into their culture.

- **Participate in local traditions:** Wroclaw has its unique customs and traditions that are celebrated throughout the year. For example, during Easter, you can join in the tradition of Śmigus-Dyngus, where people playfully splash water on each other. During Christmas, visit the festive markets and partake in the holiday traditions like decorating Christmas trees and trying traditional sweets. Participating in these traditions allows you to connect with the local community and experience their cultural practices firsthand.

- **Interact with locals:** Engaging with locals is one of the best ways to truly experience the local culture. Strike up conversations with Wroclaw residents, ask for recommendations, and show genuine interest in their stories and experiences.

Whether it's chatting with shop owners, attending community events, or joining local interest groups, building connections with locals will enrich your understanding of Wroclaw's culture and provide a unique perspective on the city.

By engaging with the local culture in Wroclaw, you'll go beyond surface-level tourism and create authentic experiences. Embrace the traditions, arts, and customs of the city, and engage with the people who call Wroclaw home. These interactions will foster meaningful connections, broaden your perspective, and leave you with a deeper appreciation for the rich cultural tapestry of Wroclaw.

By following these dos, you can embrace the local culture, connect with the people of Wroclaw, and create lasting memories of your visit. Respectful interactions, an open mind, and a willingness to experience the city beyond the surface will enrich your time in Wroclaw and leave you with a truly memorable travel experience.

Don'ts in Wroclaw

While visiting Wroclaw, it's important to be aware of the local customs and practices to ensure a respectful and enjoyable experience. Understanding the don'ts will help you navigate the city with cultural sensitivity and avoid inadvertently causing offense or discomfort. Here are some important guidelines to keep in mind during your visit to Wroclaw.

❖ Don't smoke in prohibited areas

Smoking is not allowed in many public places in Wroclaw, including restaurants, bars, public transportation, and enclosed spaces. Respect the designated smoking areas or step outside to smoke if permitted. Be mindful of others who may be sensitive to smoke or trying to enjoy a smoke-free environment. Here are some additional details on why it's essential to adhere to smoking restrictions:

- **Respect for non-smokers:** Smoking in prohibited areas can cause discomfort and annoyance to non-smokers who may be sensitive to smoke or prefer a smoke-free environment. By refraining from smoking in designated no-smoking zones, you show respect for the rights and preferences of others.

- **Compliance with local laws:** Smoking bans in public spaces, including indoor areas such as restaurants, bars, and public transportation, are typically enforced by local laws and regulations. Violating these laws can result in fines or penalties. It's important to familiarize yourself with the specific smoking regulations in Wroclaw and abide by them to avoid any legal consequences.

- **Health and safety considerations:** Smoking in crowded areas or enclosed spaces can pose health and safety risks. Second-hand smoke can be harmful to those nearby, including children, the elderly, and individuals with respiratory conditions. Additionally, smoking in prohibited areas increases the risk of accidental fires and compromises the safety of others.

- **Setting a positive example:** By refraining from smoking in prohibited areas, you set a positive example for others, including children and young adults. Demonstrating responsible behavior encourages a healthier and more considerate environment for everyone.

- **Alternative smoking areas:** If you are a smoker, Wroclaw provides designated smoking areas where you can enjoy your cigarette without infringing on the rights of non-smokers. Look for designated smoking zones, which are typically marked with signage or indicated by ashtrays. Using these designated areas ensures that you can smoke without causing inconvenience or discomfort to others.

- **Social etiquette:** Smoking in prohibited areas is generally considered impolite and disrespectful. Being mindful of your surroundings and adhering to smoking restrictions is a way to demonstrate good manners and cultural sensitivity.

Remember to familiarize yourself with Wroclaw's specific smoking regulations, which may vary in different locations, such as parks, outdoor seating areas, and public squares. Respecting these regulations not only shows consideration for others but also helps create a more pleasant and inclusive environment for everyone in Wroclaw.

❖ Don't assume everyone speaks English fluently

While English is commonly spoken in tourist areas, it's not safe to assume that everyone you encounter will be fluent in English. It's always helpful to learn a few basic Polish phrases or carry a pocket phrasebook to facilitate communication. Making an effort to communicate in the local language, even if it's just a few words, shows respect and can enhance your interactions with locals. Here are some additional details on why you should avoid making assumptions about language proficiency:

- **Cultural respect:** Respecting the local language and culture is an important aspect of being a responsible traveler. Making an effort to learn a few basic Polish phrases, such as greetings, thank you, and please, shows respect and appreciation for the local culture. It also demonstrates that you value the local language and are willing to engage with the community on their terms.

- **Enhanced communication:** Not assuming English fluency encourages effective communication and can help you navigate various situations more smoothly. Learning a few key phrases in Polish can make a significant difference in interactions with locals, particularly in less touristy areas or when seeking assistance from individuals who may not be proficient in English. It can also foster a more genuine connection with the locals, as they appreciate the effort made to communicate in their language.

- **Cultural immersion:** Engaging with the local language opens doors to a deeper cultural immersion. It allows you to better understand the local customs, traditions, and way of life. Interacting with locals in their native language can lead to more meaningful experiences, as it provides an opportunity to engage in conversations, learn about local recommendations, and gain insights into the local culture.

- **Overcoming language barriers:** By not assuming English fluency, you are better prepared to navigate situations where language barriers may arise. It encourages patience, adaptability, and a willingness to find alternative means of communication, such as using translation apps, hand gestures, or visual aids. Embracing these methods of communication can lead to interesting and memorable encounters, even when verbal language may be limited.

- **Cultural exchange:** Engaging with locals in their native language opens the door to cultural exchange. It allows for a more authentic and meaningful exchange of ideas, perspectives, and experiences. Locals may be more inclined to share their insights, stories, and recommendations when they see your genuine effort to communicate in their language.

Remember, even if your attempts to communicate in Polish are met with responses in English, your effort to bridge the language gap is appreciated. Approach each interaction with a respectful and open mindset, and be prepared to adapt to different language abilities. By avoiding assumptions about English fluency, you demonstrate cultural sensitivity, foster meaningful connections, and enhance your overall travel experience in Wroclaw.

❖ **Don't discuss sensitive topics**

Discussing sensitive topics can sometimes lead to misunderstandings or uncomfortable situations, especially when you are visiting a new destination like Wroclaw. It's important to be aware of the local customs and sensitivities, and to approach conversations with respect and cultural sensitivity. Here are some key reasons why it's advised not to discuss sensitive topics:

- **Respect for Differences:** Every culture has its own unique history, values, and perspectives. Discussing sensitive topics such as politics, religion, or historical conflicts without a deep understanding of the local context can unintentionally offend or create tension. By avoiding these discussions, you show respect for the diverse viewpoints and experiences of the local community.

- **Preservation of Positive Atmosphere:** Sensitivity towards sensitive topics helps maintain a positive and harmonious atmosphere during your visit. Traveling is an opportunity to connect with people, learn from different cultures, and build bridges. Focusing on more neutral subjects allows for open and enjoyable conversations that foster cultural exchange and understanding.

- **Avoiding Misinterpretation:** Engaging in discussions about sensitive topics without a comprehensive understanding of the local context can lead to misinterpretation or misrepresentation of viewpoints. This can result in misunderstandings or perpetuate stereotypes. It's important to approach conversations with humility and a willingness to learn, avoiding assumptions or generalizations.

- **Cultural Sensitivity:** Demonstrating cultural sensitivity is crucial when engaging with locals. Sensitive topics often involve deeply held beliefs, values, or historical events. Approaching these subjects without proper understanding can be disrespectful and insensitive. By avoiding sensitive discussions, you show consideration for the emotions and experiences of others.

- **Focus on Shared Experiences:** Instead of discussing sensitive topics, focus on topics that encourage cultural exchange, appreciation, and understanding. Engage in conversations about local traditions, customs, cuisine, or arts. This allows for a positive exchange of experiences and promotes a sense of unity and connection.

Remember, the goal of travel is to broaden our horizons, learn from different cultures, and foster positive connections. By refraining from discussing sensitive topics, you demonstrate respect, cultural awareness, and an openness to embracing new experiences. Embrace the opportunity to engage with the local community in a positive and inclusive manner, creating memorable and enriching experiences during your visit to Wroclaw.

❖ Don't be excessively loud or disruptive

Wroclaw is a vibrant city with a lively atmosphere, but it's important to be mindful of your noise levels, especially in public spaces, residential areas, and during late hours. Respect the peace and privacy of others by keeping your volume at a considerate level and avoiding unnecessary disturbances. Here are some additional reasons why it's advised not to be excessively loud or disruptive:

- **Respect for Others:** Wroclaw is a vibrant city with diverse residents and visitors. By being mindful of your noise levels, you show respect for the comfort and well-being of those around you. Whether you're in public spaces, restaurants, cafes, or residential areas, keeping your volume at a considerate level ensures that others can enjoy their surroundings without unnecessary disturbances.

- **Preserving Tranquility:** Many people visit Wroclaw to experience its charm, relax in its parks, or explore its historical sites. Excessive noise or disruptive behavior can disrupt the tranquility of these spaces and diminish the overall experience for others. By being mindful of your actions and keeping noise levels appropriate, you contribute to maintaining the peaceful ambiance that Wroclaw offers.

- **Cultural Etiquette:** Different cultures have varying expectations when it comes to noise levels and appropriate behavior in public spaces. Being aware of and adapting to the cultural norms of Wroclaw shows respect for the local customs and helps you integrate more seamlessly into the community. It also demonstrates your willingness to embrace and appreciate the local way of life.

- **Consideration for Residents:** Wroclaw is not just a tourist destination; it is a thriving city with residents who work, study, and live their daily lives there. Being excessively loud or disruptive can disrupt the peace and quiet that residents require for their well-being. By being mindful of your noise levels, especially in residential areas, you show consideration for the local community.

- **Enhancing Your Experience:** By maintaining an appropriate noise level and avoiding disruptive behavior, you create an environment that fosters positive interactions and enjoyable experiences. It allows you to fully appreciate the surroundings, engage in meaningful conversations, and connect with the local culture. Being mindful of your behavior enhances your own travel experience by creating a more harmonious and welcoming atmosphere.

Remember, Wroclaw is a city where people live, work, and enjoy their daily lives. By being aware of your noise levels, respecting cultural norms, and considering the experiences of others, you can contribute to a positive and enjoyable environment for everyone. Embrace the opportunity to immerse yourself in the local culture and appreciate the beauty of Wroclaw while being considerate of those around you.

❖ Don't disrespect religious sites and customs

When visiting religious sites in Wroclaw, such as churches or cathedrals, show reverence and respect for the sacred nature of these places. Avoid loud conversations, use of flash photography, or inappropriate behavior. Adhere to any specific rules or dress codes outlined at the entrance to ensure a respectful visit. Here are some additional reasons why it's advised not to disrespect religious sites and customs:

- **Sacredness and Significance:** Religious sites, such as churches, cathedrals, or temples, are places of worship and hold great importance to the local community. They are spaces where individuals seek solace, reflection, and spiritual connection. Disrespectful behavior, such as loud conversations, disruptive activities, or failure to adhere to specific rules or dress codes, disregards the sacredness of these places and can be deeply offensive to those who hold them dear.

- **Cultural Heritage:** Religious sites often embody significant historical, architectural, and artistic elements. They represent the cultural heritage of a community, showcasing intricate craftsmanship and centuries-old traditions. By showing respect and admiration for these spaces, you acknowledge and appreciate the cultural and artistic contributions they hold, contributing to the preservation of local heritage.

- **Customs and Rituals:** Observing customs and rituals associated with religious sites demonstrates cultural sensitivity and an appreciation for local traditions. When visiting religious sites, it's essential to follow any guidelines or instructions provided, such as removing your shoes, covering your shoulders, or refraining from photography during religious ceremonies. Adhering to these practices shows respect for the religious customs and allows others to worship without disruption.

- **Sensitivity to Believers:** Disrespectful behavior in religious spaces can deeply hurt the sentiments of believers. It's important to remember that these sites are active places of worship, and visitors should act in a manner that does not interfere with the religious experience of others. Keeping noise levels low, refraining from unnecessary conversations, and avoiding any behavior that may be deemed disrespectful ensures that everyone can worship or reflect in a peaceful environment.

- **Building Cultural Understanding:** Engaging with religious sites and customs provides an opportunity to learn about different belief systems and cultural practices. By approaching these sites with respect and an open mind, you can gain insights into the local culture, traditions, and spiritual values. Building cultural understanding fosters tolerance, empathy, and a deeper appreciation for the diversity of human experiences.

Remember, when visiting religious sites in Wroclaw, be mindful of your actions, dress modestly, and follow any specific guidelines or rules provided. By respecting the sanctity of these spaces and appreciating the cultural and spiritual significance they hold, you contribute to a harmonious environment and promote cultural exchange.

Embrace the opportunity to learn, reflect, and connect with the rich religious heritage of Wroclaw with reverence and respect.

Being aware of these don'ts, you can navigate Wroclaw with cultural sensitivity, show respect for local customs, and contribute to a positive and harmonious environment during your time in the city. Embrace the local customs, adhere to the guidelines, and enjoy all that Wroclaw has to offer while being a responsible and considerate visitor.

Following these dos and don'ts, you can navigate Wroclaw with cultural sensitivity and ensure a positive and respectful experience during your visit. Embrace the local customs, show respect for the traditions, and enjoy all that this charming city has to offer.

Plan your trip to Wroclaw

Embarking on a journey to Wroclaw is an exciting opportunity to explore a city rich in history, culture, and architectural splendor. To ensure a seamless and unforgettable trip, careful planning is key. This comprehensive guide will help you navigate the process, from pre-trip preparations to creating an itinerary that encompasses the best that Wroclaw has to offer.

i. **Research and Gathering Information:** Begin your trip planning by conducting thorough research on Wroclaw. Learn about the city's history, landmarks, local customs, and popular attractions. Gather information from trusted sources such as travel websites, guidebooks, and reputable blogs. Look for insights on the best time to visit, weather conditions, local events, and any specific considerations for travelers.

ii. **Determine the Duration of Your Stay:** Decide how long you intend to stay in Wroclaw. Consider the number of days you have available, as well as your interests and desired pace of exploration. Wroclaw offers a myriad of attractions, so allocating ample time ensures a more comprehensive experience. However, even a shorter visit can be rewarding if planned thoughtfully.

iii. **Set a Budget:** Establishing a budget is essential for managing expenses during your trip. Research the average costs of accommodations, meals, transportation, attractions, and souvenirs in Wroclaw. Allocate funds for each aspect of your trip, ensuring you have enough for both essential and discretionary expenses. Consider using a travel budgeting app or spreadsheet to track your spending.

iv. **Accommodation Selection:** Choose accommodations that suit your preferences and budget. Wroclaw offers a range of options, from luxury hotels to budget-friendly hostels and cozy guesthouses. Consider factors such as location, amenities, and guest reviews when making your selection. Booking in advance is recommended, especially during peak travel seasons.

v. **Transportation Planning:** Research transportation options for reaching Wroclaw and getting around the city. Wroclaw has an international airport with connections to major European cities, making it accessible by air. Alternatively, train or bus travel is convenient for reaching Wroclaw from other Polish cities. Within the city, consider utilizing public transportation, including trams and buses, for cost-effective and efficient travel.

vi. **Create an Itinerary:** Crafting an itinerary allows you to make the most of your time in Wroclaw. Identify the key attractions and landmarks you wish to visit, such as the Market Square, Wroclaw

Cathedral, and Centennial Hall. Research their opening hours, admission fees, and any guided tours or special experiences they offer. Balance your itinerary with a mix of popular tourist spots and off-the-beaten-path gems to truly immerse yourself in the city's charm.

vii. **Cultural Experiences and Local Cuisine:** Wroclaw boasts a vibrant cultural scene and delicious Polish cuisine. Incorporate cultural experiences, such as attending concerts, art exhibitions, or theater performances, into your itinerary. Indulge in the local cuisine by sampling traditional dishes at local restaurants or exploring food markets. Engaging with the local culture adds depth and authenticity to your travel experience.

viii. **Travel Insurance and Safety Precautions:** Prioritize your safety by obtaining comprehensive travel insurance that covers medical emergencies, trip cancellations, and lost belongings. Familiarize yourself with local emergency contact numbers and medical facilities in Wroclaw. Adhere to common safety precautions, such as safeguarding your belongings, being cautious in crowded areas, and following any local advisories.

ix. **Learn Basic Polish Phrases:** While English is commonly spoken, learning a few basic Polish phrases can enhance your interactions and show respect for the local language. Practice greetings, thank-you phrases, and polite expressions. Locals appreciate the effort made to communicate in their language, even if only a few words are mastered.

x. **Pack Appropriately and Prepare for the Weather:** Check the weather forecast for your travel dates and pack accordingly. Wroclaw experiences distinct seasons, with warm summers and cold winters. Dress in layers, carry comfortable footwear for walking, and pack appropriate clothing for the weather conditions during your visit. Don't forget essentials such as adapters for electrical outlets if needed.

Planning your trip to Wroclaw ensures a smooth and enjoyable experience. By conducting thorough research, setting a budget, and creating a well-rounded itinerary, you can maximize your time in this captivating city. Remember to embrace the local culture, engage with the residents, and savor the rich history and beauty that Wroclaw has to offer. With careful planning, your journey to Wroclaw will be filled with unforgettable memories and immersive experiences.

Tourist visa requirements for Wroclaw

If you're planning a trip to Wroclaw, it's important to familiarize yourself with the tourist visa requirements. This comprehensive guide provides essential information to ensure a smooth visa application process without repeating words.

i. **Valid Passport:** Ensure your passport is valid for at least six months beyond your planned stay in Wroclaw. Check that it has blank visa pages for any necessary stamps.

ii. **Visa Application Form:** Complete the visa application form accurately and legibly. Provide all requested information, including your personal details, travel itinerary, and accommodation details in Wroclaw.

iii. **Passport-Sized Photos:** Attach recent passport-sized photos to your visa application form as per the specifications provided by the consulate or embassy. Typically, two identical, color photos with a white background are required.

iv. **Proof of Travel Itinerary:** Submit a detailed travel itinerary, including your planned dates of arrival and departure from Wroclaw. This can include flight reservations, hotel bookings, and a comprehensive outline of your activities and destinations within the city.

v. **Proof of Accommodation:** Provide proof of accommodation arrangements in Wroclaw, such as hotel reservations or a letter of invitation from a host or sponsor. Ensure the documentation includes your name, duration of stay, and contact details of the accommodation.

vi. **Travel Insurance:** Obtain travel insurance coverage for the duration of your stay in Wroclaw. The policy should include medical coverage, emergency evacuation, and repatriation. Ensure the policy meets the minimum coverage requirements specified by the consulate or embassy.

vii. **Financial Proof:** Demonstrate sufficient financial means to support your stay in Wroclaw. Submit bank statements or proof of employment, highlighting your ability to cover expenses such as accommodation, transportation, meals, and other incidentals.

viii. **Roundtrip Flight Itinerary:** Provide a confirmed roundtrip flight itinerary or proof of onward travel from Wroclaw. This demonstrates your intention to leave the country within the authorized visa period.

ix. **Travel Intentions:** Write a detailed cover letter explaining the purpose of your visit, your intended activities in Wroclaw, and your commitment to complying with the visa regulations. This letter should be concise, honest, and clearly express your intentions.

x. **Consular Fees:** Pay the required consular fees for the visa application process. The fees may vary depending on your nationality and the type of visa you are applying for. Ensure you have the correct payment method, such as cash or credit card, as per the consulate's guidelines.

Adhering to the tourist visa requirements for Wroclaw is crucial for a successful and hassle-free trip. Make sure to gather all necessary documentation, complete the visa application accurately, and submit your application well in advance of your planned travel dates. Remember to consult the consulate or embassy for the most up-to-date and specific visa requirements based on your nationality. With careful preparation, you'll be well on your way to exploring the captivating city of Wroclaw.

Program for visa waiver

Wroclaw welcomes travelers from various countries through its program for visa waiver. This program allows eligible individuals to visit the city for a specified duration without the need for a traditional tourist visa. This article outlines the program's key features and requirements, providing valuable information for those planning a visa-free visit to Wroclaw.

i. **Eligibility Criteria:** The program for visa waiver in Wroclaw is available to citizens of select countries who meet specific requirements. Eligibility is typically based on factors such as diplomatic relations, bilateral agreements, and reciprocal visa arrangements between the applicant's home country and Poland. Check the official websites of the Polish Ministry of Foreign Affairs or the consulate/embassy in your country to confirm your eligibility.

ii. **Duration of Stay:** Under the visa waiver program, eligible travelers are granted a specific period of stay in Wroclaw without the need for a visa. The duration may vary depending on the country of citizenship and the purpose of the visit. It is essential to check the maximum allowed stay to ensure compliance with the program's guidelines.

iii. **Permitted Activities:** Visa waiver programs usually allow travelers to engage in tourism, business meetings, conferences, or cultural exchange activities during their stay in Wroclaw. However, specific limitations may apply depending on the country of citizenship. It is essential to understand the permitted activities and any restrictions outlined by the program.

iv. **Travel Authorization:** To participate in the visa waiver program, eligible travelers must obtain travel authorization before their trip. This authorization is typically issued electronically, either through an online application system or as part of the airline check-in process. The travel authorization, often referred to as an electronic travel authorization or e-visa, serves as proof of eligibility for visa-free entry into Wroclaw.

v. **Application Process:** The application process for travel authorization under the visa waiver program is typically straightforward. Applicants are required to provide personal information, passport details, travel itinerary, and answer security-related questions. Some programs may also require payment of a processing fee. It is advisable to apply for travel authorization well in advance of the intended travel dates to allow for any processing delays.

vi. **Validity Period:** The travel authorization obtained under the visa waiver program is usually valid for a specified period. It is essential to check the validity dates to ensure they cover the planned travel period to Wroclaw. Once the travel authorization expires, travelers must leave the country or apply for an appropriate visa if they wish to extend their stay.

vii. **Compliance with Immigration Regulations:** While enjoying the benefits of visa waiver, it is crucial to comply with immigration regulations and the terms of the program. This includes adhering to the permitted duration of stay, engaging in approved activities, and respecting the laws of Wroclaw. Failure to comply with these regulations may result in penalties, fines, or restrictions on future travel.

The program for visa waiver in Wroclaw provides a convenient option for eligible travelers to explore the city without the need for a traditional visa. By understanding the program's features, eligibility criteria, and compliance requirements, travelers can plan their visit to Wroclaw with ease and enjoy the city's rich history, vibrant culture, and captivating attractions. Before making travel arrangements, it is advisable to consult official sources or contact the consulate/embassy in your country to obtain the most up-to-date information regarding the visa waiver program.

When is the best time to visit Wroclaw?

Determining the best time to visit Wroclaw depends on your preferences and the experiences you seek. Wroclaw offers something unique in every season, from vibrant festivals to tranquil winter landscapes. This guide will help you decide when to plan your trip to Wroclaw based on weather, events, and overall visitor experience.

- ✓ **Spring (March to May):** Spring in Wroclaw brings a refreshing ambiance as nature awakens from winter. The weather gradually becomes milder, with temperatures ranging from 10°C to 20°C (50°F to 68°F). It's an ideal time to explore Wroclaw's picturesque parks and gardens, such as Szczytnicki Park and the Japanese Garden, as flowers bloom and vibrant colors emerge. April and May witness the Wroclaw Good Beer Festival, offering a great opportunity to savor local brews and experience lively cultural events.

- **Summer (June to August):** Summer is the peak tourist season in Wroclaw, characterized by warm temperatures ranging from 20°C to 30°C (68°F to 86°F). The city is abuzz with outdoor activities, festivals, and cultural events. The Market Square becomes a vibrant hub with street performances and outdoor dining. Don't miss the Wroclaw Summer Jazz Festival, featuring renowned international and local artists. However, be prepared for larger crowds and higher accommodation prices during this period.

- **Autumn (September to November):** Autumn in Wroclaw is a beautiful season marked by mild temperatures ranging from 10°C to 20°C (50°F to 68°F). The city's parks and tree-lined streets transform into a captivating display of autumn colors. The International Wratislavia Cantans Festival, a renowned music festival, takes place in September and October, offering a diverse program of classical and contemporary performances. Autumn is also an excellent time to explore museums and indoor attractions.

✓ **Winter (December to February):** Winter in Wroclaw brings a magical charm with its festive atmosphere and the possibility of snow. Temperatures range from -5°C to 5°C (23°F to 41°F). The city is adorned with Christmas decorations, and the Christmas Market in the Market Square is a must-visit, offering traditional food, crafts, and a delightful ambiance. Wroclaw's numerous ice skating rinks and winter sports activities provide entertainment for both locals and visitors.

Considerations:

▪ **Weather:** The weather plays a significant role in determining the best time to visit. If you prefer milder temperatures and outdoor exploration, spring and autumn are ideal.

For warm weather and vibrant street life, choose the summer months. Winter is perfect for those who enjoy festive celebrations and unique winter activities.

- **Crowd Levels:** Keep in mind that peak tourist season (summer) attracts larger crowds, while spring and autumn offer a more tranquil and relaxed atmosphere.

- **Budget:** Accommodation and flight prices may be higher during the peak summer season, so if you're looking for more affordable options, consider visiting in the shoulder seasons or winter.

Ultimately, the best time to visit Wroclaw depends on your personal preferences and interests. Whether you're captivated by the blossoming spring, the festive spirit of winter, or the lively atmosphere of summer, Wroclaw has something   to   offer   year-round.

When to avoid visiting Wroclaw?

While Wroclaw is a captivating city with much to offer, there are certain periods when it may be less ideal to visit. Being aware of these times can help you plan your trip more effectively and avoid any potential challenges. Here are some instances when it may be best to avoid visiting Wroclaw:

i. **Major Holidays and Public Events:** Wroclaw experiences increased tourism and higher crowds during major holidays and public events. If you prefer a more peaceful and less crowded experience, it's advisable to avoid visiting during these times. Examples of such events include Christmas and New Year's, Easter, and national holidays like Independence Day (November 11th) when locals celebrate with various festivities.

ii. **Peak Summer Season:** The summer months (June to August) are the peak tourist season in Wroclaw. The city becomes bustling with visitors, and popular attractions may be crowded. Accommodation prices tend to be higher during this period, and it's advisable to book well in advance if you plan to visit in summer. If you prefer a quieter and less crowded experience, you may want to consider visiting during the shoulder seasons of spring or autumn.

iii. **Extreme Weather Conditions:** Wroclaw experiences both hot summers and cold winters. If you are not accustomed to extreme weather conditions, it may be best to avoid visiting during the height of summer or the coldest winter months. Extreme temperatures can impact your comfort and limit certain outdoor activities. Instead, consider visiting during the milder seasons of spring or autumn when the weather is more pleasant for exploration.

iv. **Local Festivals or Events:** While Wroclaw hosts a variety of exciting festivals and events throughout the year, some may attract larger crowds or impact the availability of accommodations. If you prefer a quieter visit, you may want to avoid specific dates coinciding with major festivals, concerts, or sporting events, unless attending those events is part of your travel plans.

v. **Personal Preferences and Interests:** Ultimately, the best time to avoid visiting Wroclaw depends on your personal preferences and interests. Consider what kind of experience you desire and research any potential conflicts or challenges that may arise during your intended travel dates.

Being mindful of these factors, you can plan your visit to Wroclaw at a time that aligns with your preferences and provides a more enjoyable and hassle-free experience. Remember to check specific dates, local events, and consult official resources to ensure accurate and up-to-date information for your travel planning.

When is the cheapest time to visit Wroclaw?

If you're looking to visit Wroclaw on a budget, it's essential to consider the timing of your trip. By choosing the right time, you can take advantage of lower prices for accommodations, flights, and tourist activities. Here are some suggestions for the cheapest times to visit Wroclaw:

i. **Off-Peak Seasons:** The shoulder seasons of spring (March to May) and autumn (September to November) offer more affordable prices compared to the peak summer season. During these periods, you can find discounted rates on accommodations and flights. Additionally, tourist attractions and activities may have fewer crowds, allowing you to explore Wroclaw's attractions at a more relaxed pace.

ii. **Winter Season:** Wroclaw experiences colder temperatures during the winter months (December to February), which is considered the low season for tourism. This period can offer significant savings on accommodation prices and flights, especially if you avoid visiting during the Christmas and New Year holidays. Consider exploring Wroclaw's festive markets and winter activities during this time.

iii. **Weekdays:** Visiting Wroclaw on weekdays, especially outside of holiday periods, can often lead to lower prices. Many hotels, restaurants, and attractions offer mid-week discounts or special deals to attract visitors during quieter times. By planning your visit from Monday to Thursday, you can take advantage of these cost-saving opportunities.

iv. **Booking in Advance or Last Minute:** Regardless of the season, booking your accommodations and flights well in advance or opting for last-minute deals can help you secure more affordable prices. Many hotels and airlines offer discounted rates for early bookings, while last-minute deals may become available as the travel date approaches. Flexibility with your travel dates can increase your chances of finding cost-effective options.

v. **Avoiding Major Events and Holidays:** When planning your trip, be mindful of major events, festivals, and holidays in Wroclaw that may cause an increase in prices and crowd levels. Booking your visit outside of these periods can help you secure better deals and avoid inflated prices.

Remember that prices can vary based on demand, availability, and other factors, so it's advisable to compare prices and monitor deals from various sources, including hotel and flight booking websites. By strategically choosing a time when there is less demand, you can make your visit to Wroclaw more affordable without compromising on the experience.

How to get to Wroclaw?

Wroclaw, located in western Poland, is well-connected to various domestic and international transportation networks. Whether you're traveling by air, train, bus, or car, there are multiple options to reach Wroclaw. Here's a guide on how to get to Wroclaw:

i. **By Air:** Wroclaw has its own international airport, Wroclaw Nicolaus Copernicus Airport (WRO), which offers domestic and international flights. Many major airlines operate regular flights to and from Wroclaw, connecting the city to various European destinations. From the airport, you can easily reach the city center by taxi, private transfer, or public transportation.

ii. **By Train:** Wroclaw is well-connected to Poland's extensive railway network, making train travel a convenient option. The city has direct train connections to major Polish cities, including Warsaw, Krakow, Gdansk, and Poznan.

International train routes also connect Wroclaw to neighboring countries such as Germany and the Czech Republic. Wroclaw Glowny is the main train station in the city, located in the city center and offering various facilities.

iii. **By Bus:** Wroclaw has excellent bus connections, both domestically and internationally. Numerous bus companies operate routes to and from Wroclaw, providing convenient and cost-effective travel options. The city has a central bus station, Wroclaw Główny, which is well-connected to other parts of Poland and neighboring countries.

iv. **By Car:** Wroclaw is easily accessible by car, with well-maintained road networks connecting the city to other major Polish cities and neighboring countries. The A4 motorway runs east-west, connecting Wroclaw with cities such as Krakow and Katowice to the east, and with Germany to the west. Additionally, several national roads provide access to Wroclaw from different directions. It's important to check local traffic regulations, parking options, and any toll requirements before embarking on a road trip to Wroclaw.

v. **By Ferry:** Although Wroclaw is not a coastal city, it is possible to reach it by ferry via the Odra River. River cruises and ferry services operate on the Odra, connecting Wroclaw with other cities along the river, including Berlin and Prague. This option provides a scenic and leisurely way to reach Wroclaw while enjoying the picturesque landscapes along the river.

When planning your trip to Wroclaw, consider factors such as cost, convenience, and personal preferences to choose the transportation mode that best suits your needs. It's advisable to check schedules, ticket availability, and any travel restrictions or requirements before embarking on your journey.

Monthly breakdown of the best time to visit Wroclaw with activities

Welcome to Wroclaw, a city that offers captivating experiences throughout the year. To help you plan your visit, we have provided a monthly breakdown of the best time to explore Wroclaw and suggested activities to enjoy during each month. From winter wonderland festivities to vibrant summer festivals and the colorful beauty of autumn, Wroclaw has something to offer every month. Immerse yourself in the unique charm of this city as we guide you through a year-round journey of exploration and discovery. Get ready to indulge in cultural events, explore historical sites, wander through picturesque neighborhoods, and embrace the diverse seasons that shape Wroclaw's character

January

January in Wroclaw welcomes the new year with a serene ambiance and a touch of winter magic. The city is adorned with festive decorations, creating a picturesque scene that enchants visitors. Embrace the chilly temperatures as you explore the historic landmarks and architectural gems without the crowds of the peak tourist season. Discover the hidden courtyards and passages that reveal the city's rich history and architectural diversity. Immerse yourself in the warmth of Wroclaw's cozy cafes, where you can savor traditional Polish cuisine and warm up with a cup of aromatic tea or hot chocolate. Don't miss the enchanting Christmas markets that continue into the early days of January, offering a delightful experience of shopping for unique crafts and sampling local delicacies. Engage in winter activities such as ice skating in one of the city's ice rinks, or simply take leisurely walks along the Odra River, marveling at the serene beauty of the winter landscape. January in Wroclaw offers a peaceful and charming start to the year, inviting you to experience the city's historic charm and vibrant winter atmosphere.

February

In February, Wroclaw maintains its captivating charm amidst the winter season. The city exudes a cozy ambiance, inviting visitors to explore its hidden treasures and embrace the unique experiences it has to offer. Admire the architectural wonders of Ostrów Tumski and Wroclaw Cathedral, where the serene atmosphere creates a peaceful backdrop for reflection and appreciation. Take part in cultural activities, such as visiting museums and art galleries, immersing yourself in the vibrant local art scene. Experience the warmth of Wroclaw's cafes and restaurants as you indulge in traditional Polish cuisine and savor the flavors of the region. Embrace the winter landscapes by strolling through the city's parks, witnessing the beauty of snow-covered scenery. Attend theater performances or concerts, which showcase the city's rich cultural heritage. February is a month of tranquility and cultural immersion in Wroclaw, providing an opportunity to appreciate the city's architectural splendor, artistic offerings, and the peacefulness of its winter ambiance.

March

As March unfolds, Wroclaw begins to emerge from the winter slumber, welcoming the arrival of spring with open arms. The city comes alive with a renewed sense of energy and vitality. Embrace the mild temperatures as you embark on a journey to explore Wroclaw's hidden gems, including its enchanting courtyards and passages. Wander through the historic streets of the Stare Miasto (Old Town) and admire the architectural marvels that grace the cityscape. Visit the University of Wroclaw and attend public lectures or engage in intellectual conversations with scholars and students. Immerse yourself in the cultural scene by attending art exhibitions and performances at local galleries and theaters. Take part in the Wroclaw Marathon, joining runners from around the world in this thrilling event. As nature awakens, venture to the Szczytnicki Park and the Japanese Garden, where vibrant blooms and blossoming trees paint a picturesque backdrop. March in Wroclaw offers a delightful blend of cultural experiences, architectural marvels, and the refreshing ambiance of the emerging spring season.

April

In April, Wroclaw embraces the beauty of spring as nature bursts into full bloom, offering a delightful experience for visitors. The city comes alive with vibrant colors and a renewed sense of energy. Explore the captivating Szczytnicki Park and immerse yourself in the tranquility of the Japanese Garden, where cherry blossoms create a mesmerizing spectacle. Indulge in the sensory delights of Wroclaw's culinary scene, sampling traditional Polish cuisine at local restaurants and cafes. April brings the Wroclaw Good Beer Festival, an opportunity to savor a wide selection of local brews while enjoying lively cultural events. Discover the city's architectural splendor by wandering through the Market Square, admiring the stunning facades and intricate details of historic buildings. Take advantage of the pleasant weather to embark on a bike tour, exploring the city's scenic paths and charming neighborhoods. Immerse yourself in Wroclaw's rich cultural heritage by visiting the National Museum, where fascinating exhibitions showcase the region's history and art. April in Wroclaw offers a delightful blend of natural beauty, culinary delights, cultural festivities, and architectural wonders, providing an unforgettable experience for every visitor.

May

In May, Wroclaw welcomes the arrival of spring in full splendor, offering a perfect time to explore the city's vibrant atmosphere and outdoor wonders. The city bursts with life as flowers bloom, trees blossom, and the warm weather beckons visitors to embrace the outdoors. Take a leisurely boat ride along the Odra River, soaking in the picturesque views of the city's skyline and charming bridges. Visit the iconic Centennial Hall, surrounded by beautifully landscaped grounds, and immerse yourself in its architectural grandeur. Explore the bustling Market Square, where outdoor cafes and restaurants invite you to savor the flavors of Wroclaw's culinary scene. May in Wroclaw is an ideal time to attend cultural festivals and events, such as the Wroclaw Summer Jazz Festival, where you can revel in the smooth melodies of renowned international and local artists. Discover the city's rich history by joining a walking tour, delving into the fascinating stories behind its historical landmarks and hidden corners. Embrace the pleasant weather by renting a bike and exploring Wroclaw's numerous scenic paths, parks, and green spaces. May in Wroclaw offers a delightful blend of outdoor exploration, cultural experiences, and the vibrant energy of a city in full bloom, making it an ideal time to visit.

June

June in Wroclaw ushers in the warm and sunny days of summer, providing a vibrant and energetic atmosphere for visitors to enjoy. The city comes alive with an array of outdoor activities and cultural events. Immerse yourself in the lively Market Square, where street performers entertain passersby and outdoor cafes invite you to relax and soak up the vibrant ambiance. Explore the charming neighborhood of Nadodrze and its artistic spirit, with galleries and street art adorning its streets. Attend the Wroclaw Summer Jazz Festival, a highlight of June, where world-class musicians captivate audiences with their soulful melodies. Take a leisurely stroll along the picturesque Odra River, basking in the scenic views and enjoying the cool breeze. Discover the beauty of Wroclaw's islands, such as Piasek Island and Słodowa Island, where you can relax on the riverbanks and enjoy a picnic. June is also a great time to venture beyond the city and explore the surrounding countryside, with its lush landscapes and charming villages. Engage in outdoor activities like cycling, hiking, or simply lounging in one of the city's many parks, such as Park Szczytnicki or Park Grabiszyński. June in Wroclaw offers a perfect blend of cultural experiences, outdoor adventures, and the vibrant energy of a city enjoying the peak of summer.

July

July in Wroclaw is a time of vibrant energy and endless opportunities for exploration and enjoyment. As summer reaches its peak, the city comes alive with a plethora of events and outdoor activities. Immerse yourself in the lively atmosphere of the Market Square, where outdoor cafes, street performers, and bustling crowds create a festive ambiance. Take advantage of the warm weather to explore Wroclaw's neighborhoods, such as Śródmieście, with its charming streets and historic architecture. Attend the Wroclaw Summer Jazz Festival, a renowned event that attracts talented musicians from around the world, delivering captivating performances. Explore the city's cultural scene by visiting museums and art galleries, where you can appreciate contemporary art and immerse yourself in local history. July is also a great time to enjoy the picturesque Odra River, with opportunities for boat tours, kayaking, or simply relaxing by the riverbanks. Discover the city's vibrant parks, like Park Szczytnicki and Park Południowy, where you can unwind in lush green spaces and escape the urban hustle. Additionally,

July presents an ideal time to savor the local cuisine at outdoor food festivals and events, indulging in traditional Polish dishes and international flavors. Whether you're seeking cultural experiences, outdoor adventures, or simply basking in the summer vibes, July in Wroclaw offers a vibrant and memorable experience for visitors of all interests.

August

August in Wroclaw is a month filled with warmth, sunshine, and a vibrant atmosphere that entices visitors to explore and enjoy the city's numerous offerings. As summer continues, Wroclaw offers a delightful blend of cultural events, outdoor activities, and the opportunity to bask in the city's lively ambiance. Take a leisurely boat tour along the Odra River, marveling at the picturesque views of the city's skyline and iconic bridges. Explore the charming neighborhood of Śródmieście, with its architectural wonders, trendy shops, and cozy cafes. Attend open-air concerts and theater performances, where you can immerse yourself in the rich cultural scene. Visit the Panorama of the Battle of Racławice, a captivating historical exhibition that showcases a monumental painting and offers insights into Polish history. August is also a perfect time to savor the city's culinary delights, with outdoor food festivals and events offering a variety of mouthwatering dishes and refreshing beverages. Discover the vibrant street art scattered throughout the city, adding a colorful and artistic touch to the urban landscape. Embrace the warm weather by taking advantage of the city's green spaces, such as Park Grabiszyński or Park Południowy, where you can relax, have a picnic, or engage in outdoor activities. August in Wroclaw invites you to immerse yourself in the city's dynamic energy, cultural richness, and the joyous spirit of summer.

September

September in Wroclaw ushers in the arrival of autumn, offering a pleasant and vibrant ambiance for visitors to enjoy. The city begins to transition into a tapestry of warm colors as leaves change, creating a picturesque backdrop for exploration. Take a leisurely stroll through the historic streets of the Stare Miasto (Old Town) and admire the architectural marvels that grace the cityscape. Attend the Wratislavia Cantans Festival, a renowned music event that showcases exceptional classical and contemporary performances in various venues across the city. Explore the tranquil beauty of Park Szczytnicki, where you can witness the graceful transition of nature and enjoy moments of serenity. Visit the Japanese Garden, where the autumn colors create a breathtaking display. September is also an ideal time to delve into Wroclaw's cultural scene by visiting museums and art galleries, where you can immerse yourself in the region's rich history and artistic offerings. Enjoy pleasant temperatures and embark on a bike tour along the city's scenic paths, parks, and riverbanks, taking in the beauty of the changing seasons. Indulge in traditional Polish cuisine at local restaurants, where you can savor hearty autumn dishes that reflect the flavors of the season.

September in Wroclaw offers a delightful blend of cultural experiences, natural beauty, and the serene ambiance of autumn, making it an ideal time to immerse yourself in the charm of this captivating city.

October

October in Wroclaw marks the arrival of autumn in all its splendor, offering a captivating and picturesque experience for visitors. As the leaves turn vibrant shades of red, orange, and yellow, the city becomes a haven for autumn enthusiasts. Explore the hidden gems of Przedmieście Świdnickie, with its charming streets and cozy cafes that invite you to savor the season's flavors. Take leisurely walks along the Odra River, enjoying the crisp air and admiring the reflections of autumn hues on the water. Visit the iconic Centennial Hall and its surrounding grounds, where you can witness the enchanting transformation of nature. October also offers the opportunity to delve into Wroclaw's cultural scene by attending theater performances, concerts, and film festivals that showcase local and international talent. Discover the city's rich history by exploring its museums and historical sites, such as the National Museum and the Royal Palace. October is also the perfect time to embrace the Halloween spirit, with various events and parties taking place throughout the city. Indulge in the region's culinary delights, with cozy restaurants serving hearty Polish dishes that warm the soul. Additionally, consider taking day trips to the nearby countryside, where you can immerse yourself in the breathtaking autumn landscapes and visit charming villages. October in Wroclaw offers a delightful blend of autumnal beauty, cultural experiences, and the warmth of Polish hospitality, making it an ideal time to visit and immerse yourself in the charm of this captivating city.

November

November in Wroclaw offers a unique blend of tranquility, cultural richness, and the enchanting ambiance of the approaching winter season. As autumn reaches its peak, the city takes on a captivating charm with its colorful foliage and cozy atmosphere. Take leisurely walks through the historic streets of the Stare Miasto (Old Town), where you can admire the architectural gems and immerse yourself in the city's rich history. Embrace the festive spirit as the Christmas markets open their doors, filling the air with the enticing aromas of mulled wine, gingerbread, and traditional Polish delicacies. Explore the city's cultural scene by visiting museums and art galleries, where you can discover captivating exhibitions and delve into the region's artistic heritage. Visit the National Museum, where you can deepen your understanding of Polish culture and history. November is also an ideal time to warm up with a cup of hot chocolate or coffee at the city's cozy cafes, where you can relax and indulge in the ambiance of the season. Take a moment of reflection and visit the Ostrów Tumski, the oldest part of the city, and Wroclaw Cathedral, where you can immerse yourself in the spiritual atmosphere. November in Wroclaw invites you to experience the city's cultural treasures, savor the flavors of the season, and embrace the tranquil ambiance as winter begins to unfold.

December

December in Wroclaw is a time of enchantment and festive cheer as the city transforms into a winter wonderland. Embrace the magical atmosphere as the streets and squares are adorned with dazzling Christmas lights and decorations. Explore the bustling Christmas markets, where you can immerse yourself in the spirit of the season while browsing for unique gifts and sampling traditional Polish treats. Marvel at the beautifully decorated Christmas trees that grace the Market Square and other iconic locations. Attend concerts and performances that showcase the rich musical heritage of Wroclaw, including classical ensembles and festive choirs. Take part in ice skating on the city's outdoor rinks, adding a touch of winter fun to your visit. Experience the Panorama of the Battle of Racławice, a remarkable panoramic painting that depicts a significant historical event. Delight in the culinary delights of the season, with restaurants and cafes serving hearty winter dishes and festive specialties. Visit the Ostrów Tumski, Wroclaw's oldest district, and soak in the serene ambiance of its ancient streets and historic landmarks. December in Wroclaw is a time of joy, celebration, and a sense of wonder, making it an ideal month to experience the city's festive traditions and create lasting memories.

Each month in Wroclaw offers unique experiences and activities to suit different interests. Whether you're drawn to the winter charm, the vibrant summer festivals, or the colorful autumn landscapes, Wroclaw has something to offer throughout the year. Plan your visit according to your preferences and immerse yourself in the rich cultural heritage and captivating atmosphere of this enchanting city.

4 weeks itinerary in Wroclaw perfect for first timers

Embark on an unforgettable adventure in Wroclaw, Poland, with our carefully curated four-week itinerary designed to provide first-time visitors with a comprehensive and immersive experience. From exploring historic landmarks to indulging in the local cuisine and discovering hidden gems, this itinerary will introduce you to the rich cultural heritage and vibrant atmosphere of this captivating city. Get ready to delve into Wroclaw's architectural splendor, delve into its fascinating history, and embrace its warm hospitality.

Week 1: Historic Charm and Cultural Exploration

Start your Wroclaw adventure by immersing yourself in the city's rich history and vibrant cultural scene. During this week, you'll explore the historic charm of the Stare Miasto (Old Town), visit iconic landmarks, and delve into the local culture.

Day 1:

Begin your exploration at the Market Square, the heart of Wroclaw's Old Town. Marvel at the impressive Gothic-style architecture, including the Gothic Hall and the Old Town Hall, while strolling through the vibrant square. Visit the Wroclaw Cathedral, an architectural masterpiece known for its stunning stained glass windows and panoramic views of the city from its tower. Explore the tranquil ambiance of Ostrów Tumski, the oldest part of Wroclaw, which houses numerous historical buildings and churches.

Day 2:

Immerse yourself in Wroclaw's cultural scene by visiting the National Museum. Admire the vast collection of Polish art, historical artifacts, and interactive exhibitions that provide insights into the city's past. Explore the Museum of Architecture, located in the historic Arsenal building. Learn about the architectural development of

Wroclaw and discover the unique styles that define the city's skyline.

Day 3:

Take a guided walking tour to learn about the fascinating history and legends of Wroclaw. Explore the charming streets and hidden corners, while your knowledgeable guide shares stories and anecdotes about the city's past. Visit the Racławice Panorama, a remarkable circular painting that depicts the Battle of Racławice. Be captivated by the immersive experience as you step into the panoramic artwork and relive the historic battle.

Day 4:

Dive into the local cuisine by sampling traditional Polish dishes at local restaurants. Indulge in pierogi (dumplings), żurek (sour rye soup), and oscypek (smoked cheese) to experience the flavors of Wroclaw. Attend a cultural performance, such as a ballet or opera, at the Wroclaw Opera House or one of the city's theaters. Immerse yourself in the artistic talent that thrives within Wroclaw's cultural institutions.

Day 5:

Explore the historic University of Wroclaw campus, renowned for its beautiful architecture and vibrant academic atmosphere. Walk through its courtyards and visit the university's main building, the Aula Leopoldina. End your week by experiencing the vibrant nightlife in the Market Square. Visit local bars and pubs to enjoy a refreshing Polish beer or cocktail while soaking in the lively atmosphere.

During Week 1, you'll uncover the historic charm of Wroclaw's Old Town, immerse yourself in its cultural treasures, and savor the flavors of Polish cuisine. Get ready for an enriching journey that will leave you captivated by the city's rich heritage and cultural vibrancy.

Week 2: Iconic Landmarks and Hidden Gems

During the second week of your Wroclaw itinerary, you'll discover the city's iconic landmarks and uncover hidden gems that add an extra layer of charm to your visit. From architectural wonders to unique cultural experiences, this week promises to showcase the diverse facets of Wroclaw.

Day 1:

Start your week by exploring the iconic Centennial Hall, a UNESCO World Heritage site. Marvel at its impressive architecture and learn about its historical significance as you stroll through its surrounding grounds and enjoy the tranquil atmosphere of Szczytnicki Park. Visit the Multimedia Fountain, located near Centennial Hall. Be mesmerized by the synchronized water, light, and music shows that take place in the evenings, creating a dazzling spectacle.

Day 2:

Embark on a journey to discover Wroclaw's hidden courtyards and passages. Wander through charming alleyways, where you'll stumble upon cozy cafes, boutique shops, and vibrant street art. Visit the Four Denominations District, known for its multicultural heritage and diverse religious sites. Explore the stunning architecture of the White Stork Synagogue, the St. Mary Magdalene Church, and the Orthodox Church of St. Mary Magdalene.

Day 3:

Explore the Wroclaw Zoo, a delightful attraction for animal lovers. Encounter a wide range of species, from exotic animals to local wildlife, while strolling through beautifully landscaped exhibits. Take a relaxing boat tour along the Odra River, admiring the city's picturesque bridges, riverside architecture, and lush greenery. Learn about the city's history and landmarks as you cruise along the water.

Day 4:

Venture to the southern part of Wroclaw and discover the stunning Park Południowy (South Park). Enjoy a peaceful walk through its scenic trails, relax by the ponds, and admire the diverse flora and fauna. Visit the Hala Stulecia, a historic hall with a captivating architecture that hosts various events and exhibitions throughout the year. Explore its surroundings and appreciate its grandeur.

Day 5:

Uncover the fascinating history depicted in the Panorama of the Battle of Racławice, an immersive painting that showcases a significant event in Polish history. Marvel at the attention to detail and the realistic representation of the battle scene. End your week by exploring the vibrant neighborhood of Nadodrze. Admire the captivating street art that adorns the walls, visit unique shops and galleries, and relax at trendy cafes that exude a bohemian atmosphere.

During Week 2, you'll witness the architectural splendor of Centennial Hall, discover hidden courtyards and passages, and explore the city's vibrant neighborhoods. This week will leave you enchanted by the city's diverse landmarks and the charm of its lesser-known gems. Get ready to uncover the captivating layers of Wroclaw's cultural tapestry.

Week 3: Neighborhood Exploration and Outdoor Adventures

During the third week of your Wroclaw itinerary, you'll venture beyond the city center to explore the vibrant neighborhoods and engage in outdoor adventures. From serene parks to scenic bike rides, this week promises exciting experiences that showcase the natural beauty and local charm of Wroclaw.

Day 1:

Begin your week by exploring the charming neighborhood of Nadodrze. Wander through its streets adorned with colorful street art, visit unique boutiques, and unwind at cozy cafes that exude a bohemian atmosphere. Discover the Museum of Contemporary Art, located in the neighborhood, where you can admire thought-provoking contemporary artworks and gain insight into the city's modern artistic scene.

Day 2:

Immerse yourself in nature at Park Szczytnicki, a lush green oasis in the heart of Wroclaw. Take a leisurely stroll through its serene paths, relax by the ponds, and appreciate the beauty of its manicured gardens. Visit the Japanese Garden, nestled within Park Szczytnicki, and experience its tranquil ambiance. Admire the meticulously designed landscape, traditional architecture, and the mesmerizing colors of autumn foliage.

Day 3:

Rent a bike and embark on a cycling adventure along the scenic paths of Wroclaw. Explore the banks of the Odra River, passing picturesque bridges and charming parks. Discover hidden corners of the city that are best explored on two wheels. Visit Park Grabiszyński, one of the largest parks in Wroclaw. Enjoy a picnic amidst its vast green spaces, take a leisurely walk, or simply relax in the serene natural surroundings.

Day 4:

Explore the Wroclaw University campus, known for its architectural beauty and vibrant academic atmosphere. Wander through its courtyards, soak in the intellectual energy, and perhaps attend a public lecture or event. Discover the charm of the Daliowa Island, located in the Odra River. Cross the pedestrian bridge to the island and enjoy a peaceful walk, surrounded by nature and the soothing sound of flowing water.

Day 5:

Take a trip to the picturesque Park Zachodni (West Park), located on the outskirts of Wroclaw. Engage in outdoor activities such as jogging, cycling, or simply enjoying a leisurely walk through its extensive trails. Unwind at one of Wroclaw's rooftop bars, offering panoramic views of the city. Sip on a refreshing drink while taking in the enchanting skyline and the glow of the setting sun.

During Week 3, you'll explore the vibrant neighborhoods of Wroclaw, immerse yourself in serene parks, and embark on outdoor adventures. This week will provide you with a deeper understanding of the city's local charm and its connection to nature. Get ready to embrace the refreshing outdoors and discover the hidden gems that await you in Wroclaw.

Week 4: Culinary Delights and Local Experiences

During the fourth and final week of your Wroclaw itinerary, you'll indulge in the city's culinary delights and immerse yourself in authentic local experiences. From savoring traditional Polish cuisine to exploring festive markets, this week promises a gastronomic and cultural journey you won't forget.

Day 1:

Begin your culinary adventure by visiting the Hala Targowa, a bustling food market where you can sample a wide variety of fresh local produce, regional specialties, and artisanal products. Enjoy a traditional Polish breakfast at a local cafe, savoring freshly baked pastries, aromatic coffee, and perhaps trying the beloved Polish dish, scrambled eggs with kielbasa.

Day 2:

Join a cooking class to learn the secrets of Polish cuisine firsthand. Under the guidance of skilled chefs, prepare and taste dishes like pierogi (dumplings), bigos (hunter's stew), and szarlotka (apple pie). Visit a local vodka bar to experience the rich tradition of Polish vodka. Taste different varieties, learn about the distillation process, and discover the cultural significance of this iconic drink.

Day 3:

Explore the city's diverse culinary scene by dining at local restaurants. Indulge in regional delicacies like żurek (sour rye soup), gołąbki (stuffed cabbage rolls), and placki ziemniaczane (potato pancakes). Visit a traditional milk bar, where you can enjoy affordable and authentic Polish dishes that have been a staple of the local dining scene for generations.

Day 4:

Experience the festive atmosphere of the Christmas markets, which typically open in late November. Sample traditional holiday treats like pierniki (gingerbread), oscypek (smoked cheese), and mulled wine. Browse through the market stalls and shop for unique handcrafted gifts, ornaments, and souvenirs that reflect the local craftsmanship and artistic traditions.

Day 5:

Visit a local brewery to taste craft beers brewed in Wroclaw. Learn about the brewing process, sample different beer styles, and discover the thriving beer culture in the city. Take part in a culinary walking tour, where you'll explore different neighborhoods, taste local specialties, and gain insights into the city's culinary heritage and traditions.

During Week 4, you'll have the opportunity to indulge in the culinary delights of Wroclaw, from traditional Polish dishes to festive treats. Immerse yourself in the vibrant local food scene, partake in authentic experiences, and create lasting memories of the city's gastronomic offerings. Get ready to savor the flavors of Wroclaw and embrace the unique culinary traditions that make this city a food lover's paradise.

This four-week itinerary in Wroclaw is designed to provide a comprehensive and immersive experience, allowing you to discover the city's historic charm, cultural treasures, and hidden gems. From architectural marvels to culinary delights, each week offers a diverse range of activities that will leave you with cherished memories of your first visit to Wroclaw.

How to stay safe in Wroclaw

When traveling to Wroclaw, ensuring your safety and well-being is of utmost importance. Like any other city, it's essential to be mindful of your surroundings and take necessary precautions to have a secure and worry-free experience. By following some simple guidelines and staying informed, you can navigate Wroclaw with confidence and enjoy all that the city has to offer. In this guide, we will provide you with valuable tips on how to stay safe in Wroclaw, including practical advice on transportation, personal belongings, local customs, and more. Whether you're exploring the city's historic landmarks or immersing yourself in its vibrant culture, these safety measures will help ensure a smooth and enjoyable visit to Wroclaw. Here are some tips on how to stay safe in Wroclaw:

- **Be aware of your surroundings:** Stay vigilant and aware of your surroundings at all times. Pay attention to the people around you, especially in crowded areas or tourist hotspots. Avoid displaying valuable items openly, and keep your belongings secure.

- **Use reliable transportation:** When traveling around the city, use reputable and licensed taxi services or public transportation. If you prefer to walk, stick to well-lit and populated areas, especially at night.

- **Keep your belongings secure:** Pickpocketing can occur in crowded areas, so keep your belongings secure and close to you. Use a secure bag or backpack and avoid carrying large sums of cash. Consider using a money belt or a hidden pouch to store your valuables.

- **Stay connected:** Keep your mobile phone charged and have emergency contact numbers readily available. Inform a trusted person about your itinerary and check in with them regularly, especially if you're traveling alone.

Respect local laws and customs: Familiarize yourself with the local laws and customs of Wroclaw. Be respectful when visiting religious sites and adhere to dress codes if required. Avoid engaging in illegal activities and respect local traditions and customs.

Drink responsibly: If you choose to consume alcohol, do so responsibly. Excessive drinking can impair judgment and make you more vulnerable. Be cautious when accepting drinks from strangers and avoid walking alone late at night, especially in unfamiliar areas.

Use reputable accommodation: Choose reputable and well-reviewed accommodations for your stay in Wroclaw. Check online reviews, and consider booking accommodations in safe and well-traveled areas.

- **Seek local advice:** If you have any concerns or questions about safety, don't hesitate to ask locals or your hotel staff for advice. They can provide valuable insights into safe areas, transportation options, and potential risks to be aware of.

While Wroclaw is generally considered a safe city, it's always important to prioritize your personal safety and take precautions to avoid any potential risks. By staying aware, prepared, and respecting local customs, you can enjoy a safe and memorable visit to Wroclaw.

Sunburn prevention strategies for your Wroclaw trip

As you embark on your Wroclaw trip, it's important to consider the impact of the sun's rays on your skin. Wroclaw, like many other destinations, experiences sunny days, especially during the summer months, which can put you at risk of sunburn. To ensure a comfortable and enjoyable visit, it's crucial to have sunburn prevention strategies in place. In this guide, we will provide you with valuable tips and precautions to help protect your skin from sunburn during your time in Wroclaw. By following these strategies and being mindful of sun safety, you can fully appreciate the city's attractions and outdoor activities while keeping your skin healthy and protected. Here are some strategies to help you enjoy your trip to Wroclaw while keeping your skin safe:

- **Wear sunscreen:** Apply a broad-spectrum sunscreen with a high SPF (Sun Protection Factor) of at least 30 or higher. Be sure to cover all exposed skin, including your face, neck, arms, and legs. Reapply sunscreen every two hours or more frequently if you've been swimming or sweating.

- **Seek shade:** Take breaks from direct sunlight by seeking shade under trees, umbrellas, or canopies. This will help reduce your exposure to intense sunlight and give your skin a chance to recover.

- **Wear protective clothing:** Opt for lightweight, loose-fitting clothing that covers your arms and legs. Consider wearing a wide-brimmed hat to protect your face, neck, and ears. Sunglasses with UV protection are also essential to shield your eyes from the sun's rays.

- **Plan outdoor activities wisely:** Schedule outdoor activities during the early morning or late afternoon when the sun's rays are less intense. This will minimize your exposure to peak sun hours, typically between 10 am and 4 pm.

- **Stay hydrated:** Drink plenty of water throughout the day to stay hydrated and help maintain healthy skin. Avoid excessive alcohol consumption, as it can dehydrate your body and increase your risk of sunburn.

- **Be mindful of reflective surfaces:** Remember that surfaces like water, sand, and snow can reflect sunlight, intensifying your exposure. Take extra precautions by applying sunscreen more frequently and wearing appropriate protective gear.

- **Avoid tanning beds:** While it might be tempting to achieve a tan before your trip, it's important to note that tanning beds emit harmful UV radiation. Protect your skin by avoiding tanning beds altogether.

Check medication side effects: Certain medications, such as antibiotics and some topical creams, can make your skin more sensitive to sunlight. Consult with your healthcare provider or read the medication labels to understand any sun-related precautions you should take.

By implementing these sunburn prevention strategies, you can enjoy your time in Wroclaw without the discomfort and potential long-term effects of sunburn. Remember, protecting your skin from the sun is not only essential for your immediate well-being but also for maintaining healthy skin in the long run.

Best travel tips for saving money in Wroclaw

When planning a trip to Wroclaw, it's always beneficial to have travel tips that can help you save money without compromising your experience. Wroclaw offers a wealth of attractions, delicious cuisine, and cultural experiences, and with a few money-saving strategies, you can make the most of your visit while staying within your budget. In this guide, we will provide you with the best travel tips for saving money in Wroclaw, from finding affordable accommodations to exploring budget-friendly dining options and taking advantage of discounted attractions. By implementing these tips, you can enjoy a memorable and cost-effective trip to Wroclaw.

- **Plan your trip during the off-peak season:** Consider visiting Wroclaw during the shoulder seasons, such as spring or autumn, when there are fewer tourists and accommodations tend to be more affordable. Additionally, attractions and activities may offer discounted prices during these periods.

- **Look for budget-friendly accommodations:** Wroclaw offers a range of accommodation options to suit different budgets. Consider staying in guesthouses, hostels, or budget hotels, which can offer comfortable lodging at more affordable rates compared to luxury hotels.

- **Explore public transportation:** Wroclaw has a well-connected public transportation system, including buses and trams, which are not only convenient but also more cost-effective than taxis. Purchase a travel card or pass for unlimited rides within a specific duration to save money on transportation expenses.

- **Sample street food and local markets:** Indulge in the delicious Polish cuisine by trying street food options and visiting local markets. Wroclaw has a vibrant food scene, and you can find affordable and tasty dishes like pierogi, kielbasa, and obwarzanek (Polish bagels) from street vendors and market stalls.

- **Take advantage of free attractions and activities:** Wroclaw has several attractions and activities that are free to visit. Explore the Old Town, stroll along the Odra River, and visit landmarks like the Wroclaw Cathedral and the university campus, which offer stunning architecture and rich history without any admission fees.

- **Utilize discount cards and tourist passes:** Consider purchasing a Wroclaw City Card or tourist pass, which offer discounted or free entry to various attractions, as well as discounts on public transportation and dining. These cards can help you save money while exploring the city.

- **Research special discounts and promotions:** Before your trip, check for any special discounts or promotions on attractions, museums, and performances. Many venues offer reduced prices on certain days or during specific times, allowing you to experience Wroclaw's cultural offerings at a more affordable cost.

- **Plan your meals strategically:** Take advantage of affordable lunch menus or set menus offered by restaurants, which often provide a more budget-friendly dining option compared to dinner prices. Additionally, consider picnicking in parks or enjoying street food for a cost-effective meal.

By incorporating these travel tips into your Wroclaw itinerary, you can save money without sacrificing the quality of your experience. Remember to plan ahead, research discounts and promotions, and make thoughtful choices when it comes to accommodation, transportation, and dining. With these money-saving strategies, you can explore Wroclaw while staying within your budget and enjoying all that the city has to offer.

Safety on the Trail

When embarking on outdoor adventures, safety should always be a top priority. Whether you're hiking, biking, or exploring nature trails in Wroclaw, it's essential to take precautions to ensure your well-being. By being prepared and following safety guidelines, you can fully enjoy your time on the trail and minimize potential risks. In this guide, we will provide you with valuable tips and information on trail safety, including planning and preparation, equipment essentials, and emergency procedures. By prioritizing safety on the trail, you can have a memorable and worry-free outdoor experience in Wroclaw.

+ **Plan your route and check weather conditions:** Before heading out on the trail, research and plan your route thoroughly. Familiarize yourself with the trail difficulty, length, and terrain. Check the weather forecast to avoid inclement weather or potentially dangerous conditions.

- **Inform others of your plans:** Always let someone know about your hiking plans, including your intended route, expected duration, and when you expect to return. This ensures that someone is aware of your whereabouts and can raise the alarm if needed.

- **Pack essential safety gear:** Carry a well-equipped backpack with essential safety gear, including a map, compass, first aid kit, whistle, headlamp, extra clothing layers, food, water, and a multi-tool. These items can prove invaluable in case of emergencies or unexpected situations.

- **Dress appropriately and wear sturdy footwear:** Dress in layers to accommodate changing weather conditions and wear moisture-wicking clothing to stay dry and comfortable. Opt for sturdy footwear with good traction to prevent slips and falls on uneven terrain.

🔸 **Stay on designated trails:** Stick to established trails and avoid venturing off into unknown areas. Straying from marked paths can increase the risk of getting lost or encountering hazardous conditions.

🔸 **Be aware of wildlife:** When hiking in natural areas, be respectful of wildlife and maintain a safe distance. Avoid approaching or feeding animals, as this can be dangerous for both you and the wildlife.

🔸 **Stay hydrated and nourished:** Carry an ample supply of water and snacks to stay hydrated and nourished throughout your hike. Take regular breaks to rest and refuel, especially during long or strenuous hikes.

🔸 **Practice Leave No Trace principles:** Respect the environment by practicing Leave No Trace principles. Pack out all trash, avoid littering, and minimize your impact on the trail and surrounding nature.

- **Be cautious of changing conditions:** Be aware of changing trail conditions, such as slippery surfaces, steep inclines, or potential hazards. Adjust your pace accordingly and proceed with caution to avoid accidents or injuries.

- **Trust your instincts and monitor your energy levels:** Listen to your body and know your limits. If you feel fatigued or encounter unexpected difficulties, don't hesitate to adjust your plans or turn back if necessary.

- **Stay updated on local regulations:** Familiarize yourself with any specific trail regulations or guidelines provided by local authorities or park management. Adhere to these rules to ensure the safety of yourself and others.

Safety on the trail is paramount. By following these guidelines and being prepared, you can enjoy your outdoor adventures in Wroclaw while minimizing risks and maximizing enjoyment. Stay mindful, stay safe, and create lasting memories in the natural beauty of Wroclaw's trails.

Where to stay in Wroclaw?

When planning a trip to Wroclaw, one of the key decisions to make is where to stay. The city offers a range of accommodation options to suit different preferences and budgets. Whether you're looking for luxury hotels, boutique guesthouses, or budget-friendly hostels, Wroclaw has something to offer. In this guide, we will provide you with valuable information and recommendations on where to stay in Wroclaw, highlighting different neighborhoods and their unique characteristics. By understanding the options available, you can choose the perfect accommodation that suits your needs and enhances your overall experience in Wroclaw.

- **Stare Miasto (Old Town):** If you want to immerse yourself in Wroclaw's history and charm, staying in the Stare Miasto (Old Town) is a great choice. This central neighborhood is home to the Market Square, Wroclaw Cathedral, and a plethora of shops, restaurants, and attractions. Accommodation options range from luxury hotels in historic buildings to cozy guesthouses and budget-friendly hostels.

- **Nadodrze:** For a bohemian and artsy atmosphere, consider staying in the neighborhood of Nadodrze. Known for its vibrant street art, unique shops, and trendy cafes, Nadodrze offers a more alternative and eclectic vibe. Accommodations in this area often include boutique hotels, stylish apartments, and cozy guesthouses.

- **Śródmieście:** Located just south of the Old Town, Śródmieście is a bustling neighborhood that offers a mix of residential and commercial areas. Staying here provides easy access to shopping centers, restaurants, and nightlife options. You can find a range of accommodations, from mid-range hotels to serviced apartments.

Ostrów Tumski: If you prefer a quieter and more serene atmosphere, Ostrów Tumski is an excellent choice. This island neighborhood is known for its historical significance and houses several churches and religious sites. Here, you'll find charming guesthouses, bed and breakfasts, and small hotels offering a peaceful retreat.

Krzyki: Located southwest of the city center, Krzyki is a residential area that offers a mix of modern developments and green spaces. It's a great option if you prefer a quieter and more local experience. Accommodation options in Krzyki include budget-friendly hotels, serviced apartments, and guesthouses.

Przedmieście Świdnickie: Situated north of the Old Town, Przedmieście Świdnickie is a vibrant neighborhood with a mix of residential and commercial areas. It offers easy access to the city center and is known for its lively atmosphere.

You'll find a range of accommodations, from budget hotels to mid-range options.

When choosing where to stay in Wroclaw, consider factors such as proximity to attractions, desired atmosphere, and budget. It's also helpful to read reviews and research the amenities and services offered by each accommodation option. By selecting the right neighborhood and accommodation that suits your preferences, you can enhance your stay in Wroclaw and make the most of your visit to this captivating city.

Top Hotels in Wroclaw

Wroclaw offers a wide range of accommodations, including top-notch hotels that cater to various preferences and budgets. Whether you're seeking luxury, boutique charm, or budget-friendly options, the city has excellent choices to suit every traveler's needs. In this guide, we will introduce some of the top hotels in Wroclaw, known for their outstanding service, amenities, and convenient locations. From historic landmarks to contemporary design, these hotels provide a comfortable and memorable stay, ensuring a delightful experience in Wroclaw.

The Monopol Hotel

The Monopol Hotel is a prestigious five-star hotel located in the heart of Wroclaw. Housed in a beautifully restored building, this historic landmark combines timeless elegance with modern luxury. With its prime location near the Market Square, The Monopol Hotel offers guests easy access to Wroclaw's main attractions, cultural landmarks, and vibrant dining and shopping districts. The hotel's interior exudes sophistication and opulence, featuring a blend of classic and contemporary design elements. The rooms and suites are spacious, tastefully decorated, and equipped with modern amenities to ensure a comfortable and memorable stay. Guests can expect amenities such as plush bedding, flat-screen TVs, luxurious bathrooms, and complimentary Wi-Fi. The Monopol Hotel is renowned for its exceptional service and attention to detail. The dedicated and professional staff goes above and beyond to ensure that guests have a personalized and unforgettable experience. Whether you need assistance with sightseeing recommendations, restaurant reservations, or arranging transportation, the hotel's concierge service is readily available to cater to your needs. Culinary delights await guests at The Monopol Hotel's on-site restaurants. The hotel boasts a gourmet restaurant that serves exquisite Polish and international cuisine, prepared with the finest ingredients and presented in an elegant setting. Additionally, a cozy café and a stylish bar offer the perfect spaces to relax and unwind after a day of exploring the city.

For those seeking relaxation and rejuvenation, The Monopol Hotel features a wellness center complete with a sauna, fitness facilities, and a range of spa treatments. Guests can indulge in pampering experiences and enjoy moments of tranquility amidst the hustle and bustle of the city. The Monopol Hotel's historic charm, impeccable service, and prime location make it an ideal choice for discerning travelers seeking a luxurious and memorable stay in Wroclaw. Whether you're visiting for business or pleasure, this prestigious hotel promises an exceptional experience, combining elegance, comfort, and the unique charm of Wroclaw's historic surroundings.

The Granary - La Suite Hotel

The Granary - La Suite Hotel is a boutique hotel located in the heart of Wroclaw, just a stone's throw away from the vibrant Market Square. Housed in a beautifully restored granary building, this unique hotel seamlessly combines historical charm with modern design and comforts. Its central location makes it an ideal base for exploring Wroclaw's cultural treasures, architectural landmarks, and lively atmosphere. The hotel's rooms and suites are spacious, elegantly designed, and thoughtfully appointed to provide guests with a comfortable and luxurious stay. Each suite has its own unique character, featuring a blend of contemporary furnishings and elements that pay homage to the building's industrial past. Guests can enjoy modern amenities such as air conditioning, flat-screen TVs, minibars, and complimentary Wi-Fi. The Granary - La Suite Hotel offers a range of services and facilities to enhance guests' experiences. The rooftop terrace, with its panoramic views of the city, is a perfect spot to relax and enjoy the breathtaking scenery. The hotel also features a wellness center, complete with a sauna and a fitness area, providing a haven of tranquility and rejuvenation for guests.

When it comes to dining, The Granary - La Suite Hotel has a restaurant that showcases creative cuisine inspired by international and Polish flavors. The menu features a variety of dishes made from locally sourced ingredients, ensuring a memorable culinary experience. Guests can also unwind and socialize at the hotel's stylish bar, which offers an extensive selection of beverages. The attentive and friendly staff at The Granary - La Suite Hotel are dedicated to providing impeccable service and ensuring that guests' needs are met. From arranging transportation and tours to offering recommendations on local attractions and dining options, the hotel's staff is always ready to assist guests with their requests. With its blend of historical charm, contemporary design, and personalized service, The Granary - La Suite Hotel offers a unique and memorable stay in Wroclaw. Whether you're visiting for business or leisure, this boutique hotel provides a refined and comfortable oasis in the heart of the city, allowing guests to immerse themselves in the vibrant culture and beauty of Wroclaw.

PURO Wroclaw Stare Miasto

PURO Wroclaw Stare Miasto is a modern and stylish hotel located in the heart of the Old Town, offering a unique and contemporary experience for guests visiting Wroclaw. The hotel's central location provides easy access to the city's main attractions, including the Market Square, Wroclaw Cathedral, and numerous shops, restaurants, and cultural sites. The hotel's design is characterized by its sleek and trendy interiors, combining minimalist aesthetics with functional comfort. The rooms are thoughtfully designed, featuring modern furnishings, comfortable beds, and amenities such as high-speed Wi-Fi, smart TVs, and air conditioning. Each room is equipped with a tablet that allows guests to control various room functions and access useful information about the hotel and the city.

PURO Wroclaw Stare Miasto is renowned for its sustainable and eco-friendly approach. The hotel incorporates environmentally friendly practices, such as using energy-efficient systems and providing locally sourced products. Guests can appreciate the hotel's commitment to sustainability while enjoying a comfortable and contemporary stay. The hotel's communal areas are designed to foster a social atmosphere and provide spaces for relaxation and productivity. The Living Room is a vibrant and welcoming space where guests can relax, socialize, and work. It features a lounge area, co-working spaces, and a bar that serves a selection of drinks and snacks.

In addition to its stylish accommodations and communal areas, PURO Wroclaw Stare Miasto offers various services and amenities to enhance guests' stay. These include a fitness center, 24-hour reception, bike rentals, and a concierge service that can assist with tour bookings, restaurant recommendations, and other guest inquiries. PURO Wroclaw Stare Miasto's central location, contemporary design, and eco-friendly ethos make it an excellent choice for modern travelers seeking a trendy and sustainable accommodation option in Wroclaw. With its unique blend of style, convenience, and environmental consciousness, this hotel provides a comfortable and memorable stay in the heart of the city's historic charm.

The B&B Hotel Wroclaw Centrum

The B&B Hotel Wroclaw Centrum offers affordable and comfortable accommodations in a convenient location in Wroclaw. Situated in the city center, this budget-friendly hotel provides easy access to major attractions, shopping areas, and dining options, making it an ideal choice for travelers seeking value for money. The hotel features modern and well-designed rooms that provide a comfortable and functional stay. Each room is equipped with amenities such as a comfortable bed, en-suite bathroom, flat-screen TV, air conditioning, and complimentary Wi-Fi. The rooms are clean, well-maintained, and offer a cozy retreat for guests to relax and rest after a day of exploring the city. The B&B Hotel Wroclaw Centrum focuses on delivering efficient service and simplicity. The check-in and check-out processes are streamlined for convenience, allowing guests to quickly settle in and start their Wroclaw adventures. The friendly and accommodating staffs are available to assist with any inquiries or requests throughout the stay.

To cater to guests' needs, the hotel offers a buffet breakfast that provides a range of options to start the day off right. Additionally, vending machines with snacks and beverages are available for a quick and convenient refreshment option. The hotel's central location allows guests to easily explore Wroclaw's attractions on foot or by utilizing public transportation. The nearby tram and bus stops provide convenient access to various parts of the city, making it easy to navigate and discover all that Wroclaw has to offer. While the B&B Hotel Wroclaw Centrum focuses on affordability, it doesn't compromise on quality and comfort. It provides a comfortable base for travelers who prioritize convenience, cleanliness, and cost-effectiveness, allowing them to make the most of their stay in Wroclaw without breaking the bank.

The Sofitel Wroclaw Old Town

The Sofitel Wroclaw Old Town is a luxury hotel that offers a refined and elegant experience in the heart of Wroclaw's historic district. Located just steps away from the Market Square and surrounded by picturesque cobblestone streets, this five-star hotel provides a perfect blend of sophistication, comfort, and convenience. The hotel's rooms and suites are beautifully appointed, exuding a sense of timeless luxury and contemporary style. Each room is meticulously designed with attention to detail, featuring plush bedding, modern furnishings, and state-of-the-art amenities. Guests can expect amenities such as flat-screen TVs, minibars, spacious bathrooms, and complimentary Wi-Fi, ensuring a comfortable and relaxing stay. The Sofitel Wroclaw Old Town prides itself on delivering exceptional service and personalized attention to its guests. The attentive and professional staff is dedicated to ensuring that every aspect of your stay is taken care of, from assisting with check-in and providing recommendations for local attractions to catering to any special requests or requirements.

The hotel offers exquisite dining options, including a gourmet restaurant that serves a fusion of Polish and international cuisine. Guests can savor delectable dishes prepared with the finest ingredients, accompanied by a carefully curated selection of wines. Additionally, the hotel's bar offers a sophisticated setting to unwind with a signature cocktail or enjoy a selection of premium spirits. To further enhance guests' well-being, the Sofitel Wroclaw Old Town features a wellness center complete with a fitness area, sauna, and spa treatments. Guests can indulge in pampering experiences, rejuvenate their senses, and take a break from the bustling city atmosphere. With its prime location, luxurious accommodations, and exceptional service, the Sofitel Wroclaw Old Town offers an unforgettable stay in Wroclaw. Whether you're visiting for leisure or business, this upscale hotel provides a sophisticated retreat where you can immerse yourself in the city's rich history, cultural heritage, and vibrant ambiance.

The Art Hotel

The Art Hotel is a boutique hotel located in the heart of Wroclaw, known for its unique blend of art, design, and comfort. Nestled in a historic building, this hotel offers a creative and inspiring atmosphere that appeals to art enthusiasts and design lovers alike. The hotel's rooms and suites are individually decorated, showcasing contemporary artwork and stylish furnishings. Each room is a work of art in itself, with attention to detail and a focus on creating a comfortable and visually appealing space. Guests can enjoy modern amenities such as flat-screen TVs, minibars, comfortable beds, and complimentary Wi-Fi. One of the highlights of The Art Hotel is its on-site art gallery, which showcases a rotating collection of works by local and international artists. This creates a dynamic and ever-changing environment, immersing guests in a world of creativity and expression.

The hotel's restaurant offers a gastronomic experience, serving a fusion of Polish and international cuisine with an artistic twist. The menu features a range of dishes made from locally sourced ingredients, combining flavors and textures to create memorable dining experiences. Additionally, the hotel's bar provides a stylish setting to relax and enjoy a selection of cocktails, wines, and spirits.

The Art Hotel's central location allows guests to easily explore Wroclaw's attractions, including the Market Square and the Wroclaw Cathedral, which are just a short walk away. The hotel's staff is knowledgeable about the local area and can provide recommendations for cultural events, museums, and hidden gems that showcase Wroclaw's artistic and creative side.

In addition to its artistic ambiance, The Art Hotel offers practical amenities such as a fitness center, 24-hour reception, and complimentary bike rentals for guests to explore the city at their own pace. The attentive and friendly staff are always available to assist with any inquiries or requests to ensure a memorable stay. The Art Hotel is a perfect choice for travelers seeking a unique and artistic experience in Wroclaw. With its artistic flair, comfortable accommodations, and convenient location, this boutique hotel invites guests to immerse themselves in the vibrant cultural scene of the city while enjoying a truly one-of-a-kind stay

When choosing a hotel in Wroclaw, consider factors such as location, amenities, and budget. It's advisable to book in advance, especially during peak travel seasons, to secure your preferred accommodation. Whether you're seeking luxury or affordability, the top hotels in Wroclaw offer a range of options to enhance your stay and provide a memorable experience in this vibrant city.

Mouthwatering cuisine and dining you should experiences in Wroclaw

When it comes to culinary delights, Wroclaw is a city that tantalizes the taste buds with its mouthwatering cuisine and diverse dining scene. From traditional Polish dishes to international flavors, Wroclaw offers a plethora of options to satisfy every palate. Whether you're a food enthusiast, a culinary adventurer, or simply seeking a memorable dining experience, Wroclaw has something for everyone. In this guide, we will introduce you to the mouthwatering cuisine and dining experiences you should not miss while exploring the vibrant culinary landscape of Wroclaw.

Pierogi

Pierogi are a beloved and iconic dish in Polish cuisine, and no visit to Wroclaw would be complete without indulging in these delicious dumplings. Pierogi are made by wrapping pockets of dough around a savory or sweet filling and then cooking them until they are tender and flavorful. They are often served with a dollop of sour cream, melted butter, or fried onions, adding richness and enhancing their taste. The filling options for pierogi are endless, offering something for every palate. Traditional savory fillings include ruskie (potato and cheese), kapusta z grzybami (cabbage and mushroom), and mięso (meat). Each bite of these savory pierogi bursts with comforting flavors and textures. For those seeking a vegetarian or vegan option, fillings such as spinach and cheese or sauerkraut and mushroom are equally delightful. If you have a sweet tooth, don't miss the opportunity to try sweet pierogi. These delightful treats are filled with fruits such as strawberries, blueberries, or cherries, and can be enjoyed as a dessert or a sweet snack. Sweet pierogi are often sprinkled with powdered sugar and served with a drizzle of fruit syrup or a side of whipped cream. Pierogi are not only a delicious dish but also a symbol of Polish hospitality and tradition. They are often prepared during special occasions and family gatherings, and their recipes are passed down from generation to generation. In Wroclaw, you can find pierogi served in traditional Polish restaurants, as well as in local street food stalls and food markets.

To enhance your pierogi experience, consider attending a pierogi-making workshop or cooking class. These hands-on experiences allow you to learn the art of making pierogi from scratch, from preparing the dough to shaping and filling the dumplings. It's a fun and interactive way to delve into Polish culinary traditions and create memories to cherish. Whether you choose to savor the traditional savory pierogi or indulge in the sweetness of the fruit-filled varieties, pierogi in Wroclaw are a culinary delight not to be missed. So, take a bite into these pillowy pockets of goodness and let the flavors of Poland tantalize your taste buds.

Polish Soups

Polish cuisine is renowned for its hearty and flavorful soups, which play a significant role in the country's culinary traditions. Wroclaw, with its rich food culture, offers a variety of Polish soups that are sure to delight your taste buds. Here are some popular Polish soups that you should try during your visit:

i. **Barszcz (Beetroot Soup):** Barszcz is a vibrant and tangy soup made from beetroots. It can be served hot or cold and is often enjoyed as a starter or a refreshing summer dish. The soup's distinctive deep red color comes from the beets, and its flavor is enhanced with a touch of sourness from fermented beet juice or vinegar. Barszcz is typically served with a dollop of sour cream and sometimes accompanied by savory dumplings called uszka.

ii. **Żurek (Sour Rye Soup):** Żurek is a traditional Polish soup with a sour and tangy flavor. It is made from fermented rye flour, which gives the soup its distinctive taste. Żurek often contains chunks of smoked sausage, potatoes, and other vegetables. This soup is commonly enjoyed during

Easter celebrations in Poland, but you can find it throughout the year in Wroclaw's restaurants. It is typically served with a garnish of hard-boiled eggs and sometimes accompanied by a side of white sausage.

iii. **Barszcz czerwony z uszkami (Red Borscht with Dumplings):** This is a variation of barszcz that features small savory dumplings called uszka. The uszka are typically filled with a mixture of mushrooms and onions. The dumplings are added to the barszcz, creating a flavorful and satisfying combination. This dish is often enjoyed during Christmas celebrations in Poland and is a favorite among locals and visitors alike.

iv. **Rosół (Chicken Broth):** Rosół is a classic Polish chicken soup known for its comforting and nourishing qualities. It is made by simmering chicken meat and bones with vegetables, such as carrots, celery, and parsley, to create a flavorful broth. The soup is often served with homemade noodles or fine egg noodles, adding substance to the dish. Rosół is a popular choice during colder months or when you need a warm and comforting meal.

v. **Zupa Grzybowa (Mushroom Soup):** Mushroom lovers should not miss Zupa Grzybowa, a rich and earthy soup made with a variety of mushrooms. The soup typically contains forest mushrooms, such as porcini, mixed with onions, herbs, and sometimes cream. The result is a hearty and aromatic soup that captures the essence of Polish forest flavors. Zupa Grzybowa is particularly popular during the mushroom-picking season in Poland.

These are just a few examples of the delicious Polish soups you can savor in Wroclaw. Each soup offers a unique blend of flavors and ingredients, reflecting the culinary traditions and regional variations within Poland.

So, immerse yourself in the rich soup culture of Poland and let these traditional dishes warm your soul and introduce you to the authentic flavors of Polish cuisine.

Traditional Polish Cuisine

Polish cuisine is rich in flavors, hearty dishes, and a blend of ingredients that reflect the country's agricultural heritage. When visiting Wroclaw, you have the opportunity to savor traditional Polish cuisine, which showcases the essence of the country's culinary traditions. Here are some iconic dishes and flavors that you should try:

i. **Bigos (Hunter's Stew):** Bigos is a classic Polish dish that embodies the heartiness of Polish cuisine. It is a stew made with sauerkraut, various types of meat (such as pork, beef, and sausage), and a medley of spices and herbs. The dish is slow-cooked to allow the flavors to meld together, resulting in a rich and comforting stew. Bigos is often served with mashed potatoes or bread and is a staple during festive occasions.

ii. **Kielbasa:** Kielbasa refers to Polish sausages, which come in various flavors and types. They are often made from pork, beef, or a combination of meats, and are seasoned with a variety of spices. Grilled or fried, kielbasa is a popular street food and a staple ingredient in many Polish dishes. Pair it with sauerkraut and mustard for an authentic Polish flavor combination.

iii. **Golonka (Pork Knuckle):** Golonka is a tender and flavorful dish made from braised pork knuckle. The meat is slow-cooked until it becomes fall-off-the-bone tender, resulting in a dish that is both succulent and indulgent. Golonka is often served with potatoes, sauerkraut, and mustard, creating a satisfying and comforting meal.

iv. **Placki Ziemniaczane (Potato Pancakes):** Placki Ziemniaczane are crispy potato pancakes that are a popular side dish or appetizer in Polish cuisine. Grated potatoes are mixed with onions, eggs, and flour, then fried until golden and crispy. They are often served with sour cream or applesauce and make for a delicious and satisfying treat.

v. **Sernik (Cheesecake):** Polish cheesecake, known as sernik, is a rich and creamy dessert made with quark cheese, eggs, sugar, and often flavored with vanilla or lemon zest. It has a smooth and dense texture, distinct from other types of cheesecake. Sernik is a favorite among Poles, and you can find different variations of this dessert in Wroclaw's bakeries and cafes.

These are just a few examples of the traditional Polish dishes that await you in Wroclaw. Polish cuisine celebrates the use of simple ingredients, hearty flavors, and time-honored cooking techniques that have been passed down through generations. So, indulge in the flavors of Polish tradition and experience the richness of Polish cuisine during your visit to Wroclaw.

International Cuisine

Wroclaw is a city known for its vibrant and diverse culinary scene, offering a wide range of international cuisines to cater to every taste and preference. Whether you're craving Mediterranean flavors, Asian delicacies, or American classics, Wroclaw has a plethora of restaurants and eateries that serve up delicious international dishes. Here are some popular international cuisines you can explore in Wroclaw:

i.   **Italian Cuisine:** Italian cuisine is well-represented in Wroclaw, with numerous trattorias, pizzerias, and Italian-inspired restaurants throughout the city. Indulge in authentic pasta dishes like spaghetti carbonara or hearty pizzas topped with fresh ingredients. Pair your meal with a glass of Italian wine for a complete Italian dining experience.

ii. **Asian Cuisine:** Wroclaw boasts a diverse range of Asian cuisines, including Chinese, Japanese, Thai, and Vietnamese. Savor the flavors of aromatic Thai curries, indulge in sushi and sashimi at Japanese restaurants, or enjoy the delicate flavors of Vietnamese pho. You can also explore Chinese dim sum or savor the fiery Sichuan dishes.

iii. **Mediterranean Cuisine:** Mediterranean cuisine, with its focus on fresh ingredients and simple yet flavorful preparations, can be found in various restaurants in Wroclaw. Delight in the vibrant flavors of Greek moussaka, Turkish kebabs, or Spanish tapas. Enjoy dishes featuring olives, olive oil, tomatoes, herbs, and spices that capture the essence of Mediterranean cuisine.

iv. **Middle Eastern Cuisine:** Experience the exotic flavors of the Middle East in Wroclaw through Lebanese, Turkish, or Moroccan cuisine. Indulge in the aromatic spices, tender kebabs, flavorful hummus, and delicious falafel. Don't forget to try traditional Middle Eastern sweets like baklava or kunafeh for a sweet ending to your meal.

v. **American Cuisine:** If you're in the mood for American classics, Wroclaw has a range of restaurants serving up burgers, ribs, steaks, and other American favorites. Indulge in a juicy burger with all the fixings, enjoy a hearty plate of barbecue ribs, or dig into a sizzling steak cooked to perfection. Complete your American dining experience with classic sides like mac and cheese or coleslaw.

These are just a few examples of the international cuisines you can explore in Wroclaw. The city's culinary landscape offers a wide array of flavors, ingredients, and culinary traditions from around the world. So, whether you're a food enthusiast, an adventurous eater, or simply seeking a taste of home, Wroclaw's international cuisine scene has something to satisfy every palate.

Street Food

When it comes to street food, Wroclaw has a vibrant and diverse scene that caters to every taste and craving. Exploring the city's streets and food markets will reveal a myriad of delicious street food options that are perfect for a quick bite or a satisfying meal on the go. Here are some popular street food choices to indulge in while in Wroclaw:

i. **Zapiekanki:** Zapiekanki is a popular Polish street food that resembles an open-faced baguette sandwich. It is made by halving a baguette and topping it with a variety of ingredients such as sautéed mushrooms, cheese, ham, onions, and ketchup. The loaded baguette is then baked until the cheese is melted and bubbly. Zapiekanki stalls can be found in many food markets and street corners, offering a delicious and filling option for a quick meal.

ii. **Obwarzanki:** Obwarzanki are traditional Polish bagels that are boiled and then baked, resulting in a chewy texture and a golden crust. They come in different flavors and are often sprinkled with salt, sesame seeds, poppy seeds, or cheese. You can find obwarzanki at street food stalls or carts, and they make for a tasty and portable snack while exploring the city.

iii. **Oscypek:** Oscypek is a smoked cheese made from sheep's milk, originating from the Tatra Mountains in Poland. This distinctive cheese is shaped into a spindle and has a slightly salty and smoky flavor. It is often grilled or fried and served with cranberry sauce. Look for street food stalls or vendors selling oscypek to try this unique and delicious Polish delicacy.

iv.   **Kebabs:** Wroclaw's street food scene wouldn't be complete without kebabs. You can find many stalls and small eateries serving up juicy and flavorful kebabs made with tender meat (often chicken or lamb), fresh vegetables, and various sauces and spices. These portable and satisfying wraps are perfect for a quick and tasty meal on the go.

v.   **Polish Sausages:** Wroclaw's street food stalls often feature sizzling Polish sausages, known as kielbasa. These grilled sausages are typically served in a bun with mustard and sauerkraut or fried onions. Grab one of these flavorful sausages for a delicious street food experience with a Polish twist.

vi.   **Paczki:** Paczki are Polish doughnuts that are deep-fried until golden and then filled with various sweet fillings, such as jam, custard, or chocolate. They are often dusted with powdered sugar and make for a delightful treat while strolling through the city.

These are just a few examples of the mouthwatering street food options you can find in Wroclaw. Exploring the city's food markets, attending food festivals, or simply wandering through the streets will allow you to discover a wide variety of street food stalls and vendors, each offering their own tempting specialties. So, embrace the street food culture of Wroclaw and let your taste buds explore the delicious flavors that the city has to offer.

Craft Beer and Breweries

Wroclaw has a thriving craft beer scene, making it a haven for beer enthusiasts and those looking to explore the world of artisanal brews. The city is home to several craft breweries and beer bars that showcase the creativity and passion of local brewers. Here's a glimpse into

Wroclaw's craft beer culture and some of the must-visit breweries and bars:

Craft Breweries:

i. **Browar Stu Mostów:** Browar Stu Mostów is one of Wroclaw's most renowned craft breweries. They pride themselves on producing high-quality beers using traditional brewing techniques and carefully selected ingredients. The brewery offers a wide range of styles, from hop-forward IPAs to rich stouts and flavorful Belgian ales. Visitors can take brewery tours, participate in beer tastings, and even try their hand at brewing during special workshops.

ii. **Warsztat Piwowarski:** Warsztat Piwowarski is a microbrewery that embraces experimentation and creativity. They constantly push the boundaries of beer styles, resulting in unique and innovative brews. With a rotating selection of beers on tap, visitors can experience a diverse range of flavors and aromas. The brewery often hosts events and beer releases, providing an opportunity to engage with the local craft beer community.

iii. **Pracownia Piwa i Przyjaciele:** Pracownia Piwa i Przyjaciele is a cozy craft brewery located in the heart of Wroclaw. The brewery focuses on producing small-batch, handcrafted beers with a strong emphasis on quality and flavor. They offer a variety of beer styles, including pale ales, porters, and lagers. The brewery's taproom is a great place to sample their creations while enjoying the laid-back atmosphere.

Beer Bars and Pubs:

i. **Kontynuacja:** Kontynuacja is a popular craft beer bar in Wroclaw, known for its extensive selection of local and international brews. With over 20 taps, visitors can enjoy a rotating lineup of craft beers from various breweries. The bar's knowledgeable staff can guide you through their offerings, ensuring a memorable beer-drinking experience.

ii.   **Kuźnia Piwa:** Kuźnia Piwa is a craft beer pub located in the city center. This cozy establishment offers a wide range of craft beers on tap, featuring both Polish and international brews. The pub's laid-back atmosphere and friendly staff create a welcoming environment for beer enthusiasts to enjoy their favorite brews.

iii. **Zielony Kij:** Zielony Kij is a craft beer bar and bottle shop that celebrates the diversity of craft beer. They offer an extensive selection of bottled beers from Poland and around the world, allowing you to explore different styles and flavors. You can also enjoy a pint of craft beer on site while chatting with fellow beer enthusiasts.

Wroclaw's craft beer scene continues to grow, with new breweries and beer bars emerging. Whether you're a seasoned beer connoisseur or simply curious about exploring the world of craft beer, Wroclaw's craft breweries and beer establishments offer an exciting and flavorful experience. So, raise a glass, savor the unique brews, and immerse yourself in the dynamic craft beer culture of Wroclaw.

Sweet Treats

Wroclaw is a city that caters to those with a sweet tooth, offering a delectable array of sweet treats and desserts that are sure to satisfy any craving. From traditional Polish pastries to international delights, Wroclaw has something for every dessert lover. Here are some must-try sweet treats when visiting the city:

i. **Polish Pączki:** Pączki are Polish doughnuts that are deep-fried until golden and then filled with a variety of sweet fillings. Traditional fillings include rose jam, plum jam, or custard, and they are often dusted with powdered sugar. These fluffy and indulgent treats are commonly enjoyed on Fat Thursday (Tłusty Czwartek), a day dedicated to eating doughnuts before the start of Lent. However, you can find pączki in bakeries and pastry shops throughout the year.

ii. **Chruściki:** Chruściki, also known as Angel Wings or Faworki, are delicate and crispy pastries that are popular during festive occasions, such as Christmas and Easter. They are made from a dough that is rolled out, cut into ribbons or intricate shapes, and deep-fried until golden and crispy. Chruściki are often sprinkled with powdered sugar and make for a delightful treat to enjoy with a cup of coffee or tea.

iii. **Sernik:** Sernik, or Polish cheesecake, is a creamy and rich dessert made with quark cheese, eggs, sugar, and often flavored with vanilla or lemon zest. The cake has a smooth and dense texture, distinct from other types of cheesecake. Sernik can be enjoyed plain or topped with fruits, such as cherries or strawberries, and is a favorite among Poles. You can find delicious sernik in pastry shops and cafes throughout Wroclaw.

iv. **Makowiec:** Makowiec is a traditional Polish poppy seed cake that is typically served during Christmas and Easter. The cake consists of layers of sweet yeast dough filled with a mixture of ground poppy seeds, nuts, honey, and raisins. Makowiec is often rolled into a spiral shape, creating a beautiful and flavorful dessert that is enjoyed by many during the holiday season.

v. **Artisanal Ice Cream:** Wroclaw boasts several artisanal ice cream shops that offer a wide selection of creative and delicious flavors. From classics like vanilla and chocolate to unique combinations such as lavender-honey or salted caramel with pretzel, you can satisfy your ice cream cravings with the city's creamy and indulgent offerings. Look out for gelaterias and ice cream parlors that use locally sourced ingredients for an authentic and flavorful experience.

These are just a few examples of the sweet treats you can indulge in while in Wroclaw. So, be sure to leave room for dessert and explore the city's pastry shops, bakeries, and ice cream parlors to discover a world of irresistible flavors and mouthwatering treats.

Wroclaw's culinary landscape is a treasure trove of flavors and experiences. By immersing yourself in the city's vibrant dining scene, you can embark on a culinary journey that showcases the rich culinary heritage of Poland and the diverse international influences that shape Wroclaw's cuisine. So, prepare your taste buds for an unforgettable gastronomic adventure in Wroclaw, where every bite is a delight to be savored.

Nightlife and Entertainment in Wroclaw

Wroclaw comes alive at night with a vibrant and diverse nightlife scene, offering something for everyone, whether you're looking to dance the night away, enjoy live music performances, or simply relax with a drink in a cozy bar. The city's dynamic and eclectic nightlife ensures that visitors can experience a memorable and entertaining evening. From bustling clubs and trendy bars to cultural venues hosting live performances, Wroclaw has an array of options to suit different tastes. Here's a glimpse into the nightlife and entertainment scene in Wroclaw:

Nightclubs and Bars

Wroclaw boasts a variety of nightclubs and bars that cater to different music preferences and atmospheres. In the city center, you'll find vibrant clubs featuring DJs spinning the latest electronic, dance, and house music, creating an energetic atmosphere for those seeking a lively night out. These clubs often host themed parties, guest DJs, and special events to keep the party spirit alive. If you prefer a more relaxed ambiance, Wroclaw also has numerous cozy bars and lounges where you can unwind, enjoy a cocktail, and engage in conversations with friends or fellow travelers.

Live Music and Concerts

For music lovers, Wroclaw offers a thriving live music scene. You can find venues throughout the city that host a variety of performances, including rock, jazz, blues, classical, and indie music. Check out popular music clubs and concert halls that feature local and international bands, solo artists, and orchestras. These venues often showcase a mix of genres and provide an opportunity to immerse yourself in the city's vibrant music culture.

Cultural Events and Theaters

Wroclaw is known for its rich cultural heritage, and the city's theaters and cultural venues are worth exploring for an evening of entertainment. The city has a range of theaters that host performances, including plays, ballet, opera, and contemporary dance. You can also catch film screenings, art exhibitions, and other cultural events at various venues throughout the city. Keep an eye on the event calendar to see what shows and performances are happening during your visit.

Riverside Hangouts and Outdoor Bars

During the warmer months, Wroclaw's riverside becomes a popular spot for locals and visitors alike. Along the Oder River, you'll find outdoor bars, beer gardens, and pop-up venues where you can relax and enjoy a drink with scenic views. This riverside setting creates a lively and laid-back atmosphere, perfect for mingling with friends, soaking up the atmosphere, and enjoying the beauty of Wroclaw.

Alternative and Underground Scene

Wroclaw's nightlife also caters to the alternative and underground scene. There are hidden gems, underground clubs, and alternative music venues where you can experience the city's alternative music, subcultures, and artistic expressions. These venues offer a unique and edgy atmosphere, often hosting live performances, DJ sets, and artistic events that showcase the city's creative spirit.

Safety and Enjoyment

While enjoying Wroclaw's nightlife, it's important to prioritize safety and responsible behavior. Like any city, it's advisable to be aware of your surroundings, travel in groups, and take necessary precautions. Respect local customs and regulations, and drink responsibly to ensure an enjoyable and safe experience.

Wroclaw's nightlife and entertainment scene is a reflection of the city's dynamic and vibrant atmosphere.

Whether you're seeking an exciting night out, a cultural experience, or a relaxing evening with friends, Wroclaw offers an array of options to suit your preferences. So, get ready to explore the city after dark and create lasting memories in Wroclaw's energetic and diverse nightlife.

Wroclaw packing list

Planning a trip to Wroclaw requires careful consideration of what to pack to ensure a comfortable and enjoyable stay. Wroclaw's diverse attractions, weather conditions, and cultural experiences call for a well-thought-out packing list. From essential clothing items to practical accessories, here are some items to consider including in your packing list for Wroclaw:

- **Weather-Appropriate Clothing:** Wroclaw experiences distinct seasons, so it's important to pack clothing suitable for the weather during your visit. In summer (June to August), pack lightweight and breathable clothing such as t-shirts, shorts, skirts, and dresses. Spring and autumn (April to May and September to October) may require layering options with light jackets or sweaters for cooler temperatures. Winters (December to February) can be cold, so pack warm clothing including a heavy coat, hats, scarves, and gloves.

- **Comfortable Walking Shoes:** Wroclaw is a walkable city with cobblestone streets and numerous attractions to explore on foot. Make sure to pack comfortable walking shoes or sneakers to ensure comfort while sightseeing. Opt for shoes with good arch support and cushioning to make the most of your explorations without discomfort.

- **Travel Adapter and Electronics:** Remember to pack a travel adapter suitable for the type of electrical outlets used in Poland. This will allow you to charge your electronic devices such as smartphones, cameras, and laptops. It's also helpful to pack a portable charger to ensure your devices stay powered throughout the day.

- **Day Bag or Backpack:** A day bag or backpack is essential for carrying your daily essentials while exploring Wroclaw. Choose a bag that is comfortable to carry and has enough space for your belongings, including a water bottle, snacks, camera, maps, and any other items you may need throughout the day.

- **Travel Documents and Essentials:** Don't forget to pack your travel documents, including your passport, identification cards, travel insurance information, and any necessary visas. It's also advisable to have printed copies or digital backups of these documents. Additionally, include any necessary medication, prescriptions, or personal care items that you may require during your trip.

- **Umbrella or Raincoat:** Wroclaw experiences occasional rainfall throughout the year, so it's a good idea to pack a compact umbrella or a lightweight raincoat to stay dry during unexpected showers.

- **Language Guidebook or Translation App:** While English is spoken in many tourist areas, having a language guidebook or translation app can be helpful for basic communication and understanding local customs. It's always nice to learn a few essential Polish phrases to enhance your interactions with locals.

Remember to pack according to your personal needs and the specific activities you plan to undertake during your visit to Wroclaw. Checking the weather forecast before your trip can help you pack appropriately. Packing light, versatile, and comfortable items will ensure you have an enjoyable and hassle-free experience in Wroclaw.

Conclusion

Wroclaw is a captivating destination that seamlessly blends history, culture, and natural beauty. This travel guide has provided you with a comprehensive overview of what makes Wroclaw a must-visit city. From its rich history and stunning architecture to its vibrant cultural scene and delectable cuisine, Wroclaw offers something for every traveler. Explore the city's historic charm by wandering through its picturesque streets, admiring its iconic landmarks like the Market Square and Wroclaw Cathedral. Immerse yourself in the local culture by visiting museums, attending cultural events, and indulging in traditional Polish cuisine.

Venture beyond the city center to discover hidden gems and neighborhoods that offer a different perspective of Wroclaw. Whether it's the artistic vibe of Nadodrze, the modern architecture of Przedmieście Świdnickie, or the tranquil atmosphere of Ostrów Tumski, each neighborhood has its own unique character and charm. When it comes to entertainment, Wroclaw's nightlife and live music scene provide endless options for fun and excitement. Dance the night away in trendy clubs, savor craft beers in lively pubs, or enjoy live performances at theaters and music venues. To ensure a smooth and enjoyable trip, familiarize yourself with practical information such as visa requirements, local customs, and transportation options. Keep in mind the best time to visit Wroclaw based on your preferences and the activities you wish to engage in.

As you embark on your journey to Wroclaw, be open to new experiences, interact with the friendly locals, and embrace the city's unique atmosphere. Wroclaw is ready to welcome you with open arms and offer a memorable travel experience filled with history, culture, and warmth. So pack your bags, prepare to explore, and create lasting memories in the enchanting city of Wroclaw.